LIVING
APOCALYPSE

A Revelation Reader and
A Guide for the Perplexed

GREGORY J. LAUGHERY

destinēe

© 2008 & 2018 Gregory J. Laughery

Without limiting the rights under copyright reserved above, no part of this publication may be reproduced, stored in, or introduced into a retrieval system, or transmitted in any form or by any means (electronic, mechanical, photocopying, or otherwise), without the prior written permission from the publisher, except where permitted by law, and except in the case of brief quotations embodied in critical articles and reviews. For information, write: info@destinee.ch

Reasonable care has been taken to trace original sources and copyright holders for any quotations appearing in this book. Should any attribution be found to be incorrect or incomplete, the publisher welcomes written documentation supporting correction for subsequent printing.

Some Scripture quotations are taken from the Holy Bible, New International Version®. NIV®. Copyright ©1973, 1978, 1984 by International Bible Society.
Used by permission of Zondervan. All rights reserved.
Other Scripture quotations are taken from New Revised Standard Version of the Bible, copyright © 1989 by the Division of Christian Education of the National Council of the Churches of Christ in the USA. Used by permission. All rights reserved.

Published by Destinée S.A., www.destinee.ch
Copy editing by Erin Hobbie and Renea McKenzie
All rights reserved by the author.

ISBN 978-0-9759082-8-0

CONTENTS

Acknowledgments   v
Abbreviations   vii

1. Introduction   1
2. Prologue (1:1-20)   6
3. The Seven Letters (2:1-3:22)   18
4. The Heavenly Court, the Lamb, & the Scroll (1) (4:1-5:14) 50
5. The Heavenly Court, the Lamb & the Scroll (2) 4:1-5:14   56
6. Opening the Six Seals (6:1-17)   61
7. Two Multitudes (7:1-17)   66
8. The Seventh Seal & the Six Trumpets (1) (8:1-9:21)   73
9. The Seventh Seal & the Six Trumpets (2) (8:1-9:21)   79
10. The Little Scroll (10:1-11)   84
11. Two Witnesses & the Seventh Trumpet (11:1-19)   89
12. The Woman, Her Son & the Dragon (12:1-17)   99
13. Two Beasts (13:1-18)   107
14. Vindication & Judgement (14:1-20)   114
15. The Seven Angels & the Last Plagues (15:1-8)   124
16. The Seven Bowls (16:1-20)   128
17. The Woman, Wisdom, & Victory for The Lamb (17:1-18) 135
18. Babylon Falls (18:1-24)   143
19. Hallelujah & the Rider on the White Horse (19:1-21)   149
20. A Thousand Years (20:1-15)   157
21. The New Heavens & New Earth (21:1 - 22:21)   169

Select Bibliography   181

ACKNOWLEDGMENTS

I am grateful to my editors Erin Hobbie and Renea McKenzie for doing their work with, patience, grace, and diligence. Their thoughts, ideas, and corrections helped in numerous ways to make this text so much better than it ever was. They are a remarkable duet, and it has been a joy to share community life with them for a season.

Sincere thanks go to Dr. Ralph McCall. Destinée has also published my book *Living Spirituality: Illuminating the Path* and enthusiastically supported this project from the beginning. Merci Ralph.

My debt to commentators on the book of Revelation is evident in these pages, and especially so to those mentioned in the Select Bibliography. I thank them all for their dedication, insights, and hard work.

ABBREVIATIONS

Biblical Literature

Col.	Colossians	Jer.	Jeremiah
		Jn.	John
1 Cor.	1 Corinthians	Lev.	Leviticus
2 Cor.	2 Corinthians	Mat.	Matthew
Dan.	Daniel	Num.	Numbers
Eph.	Ephesians	Phil.	Philippians
Ex.	Exodus	Ps.	Psalm
Ezk.	Ezekiel	Rev.	Revelation
Gen.	Genesis	Rom.	Romans
Hab.	Habakkuk	Zech.	Zechariah
Heb.	Hebrews		
Hos.	Hosea		
Isa.	Isaiah		
Jas.	James		

Other Abbreviations

Cf.   consult
ff   following pages or verses

INTRODUCTION

Everybody is interested in the subject of the end of the world. As any internet search engine will show, there is an astronomical number of entries on this topic. Curiosity drives us towards seeking to understand what the future holds for ourselves and the world, and there is definitely no shortage of books, websites, or blogs that attempt to predict it for us.

We live in a world where wars and rumors of wars proliferate, the threat of nuclear devastation and climate calamities multiply, genocide and racism flourish, and dictators dominate and destroy their people; meanwhile, peace, progress, technology, and prosperity seem to steam ahead in a unperturbed manner. Furthermore, today we face the risk of a financial meltdown, are plagued by a massive housing crisis, and continue to be enslaved to spiraling oil prices.

For many people, these pervasive tendencies are an indication that we are living in the last days. Time is running out, and the denouement is at hand. How are we to respond? What is our part in the unfolding story? We desperately long to see ahead to next week, to next year, and eventually to where our final destiny lies, as the reality of death looms over us all. We all want to know if the world will ever end and what will happen to us if it does?

The book of Revelation offers acute and compelling responses to the previous questions, as well raising a host of others. This remarkable text contains mysterious codes, highly symbolic imagery, significant turning points in time, shifts of historical perspective, and a mixture of heavenly and earthly visions that saturate the landscape of life and death. What might these have to do with the future of the world and our ultimate destiny?

Revelation announces that the age-long battle between good and evil is headed for a vital showdown and that God is and will be victorious as history is brought to a close. When it all comes down, and it will, we need to know whose side we're on. This means there are many important questions to be asking ourselves including: Who are we following? How are we living? And where, if anywhere, is the world going?

Several years ago, someone once told me that Saddam Hussein was the antichrist and that the end of the world was at hand. There was another prediction circulating at roughly the same time when Europe moved towards unification—the European Community was the beast. This new organization of countries was assumed to be a clear sign of the fulfillment of the end times. These sorts of preposterous predictions have side-tracked readers and not helped us better understand or live out the truth of Revelation, this relevant, frightening, and crucial part of the Scripture.

As we read the book of Revelation together, we face the challenge of avoiding wildly inaccurate assumptions and false interpretations. The aim and hope in writing *Living Apocalypse*, where *Living* resounds as both verb and adjective, is that we might discover more about how to live as followers of the crucified and risen One, grow in faith, and deeply experience the truth and wonder of the word, presence, and reality of Almighty God.

We embark on our journey with an important survey of the literary genre of Revelation, and four of the major ways which it has been interpreted. A study of genre and the forces of interpretive perspectives are always part of a valid approach to the text. Theology is interconnected with these, so we want to be aware of them.

Apocalyptic Literature

Apocalyptic literature is a term used to refer to a group of writings usually dated from around 200 BCE to 100 CE. These writings set out to explain why the arrival of the kingdom of God had been delayed or why the righteous continued to suffer in what was understood to be an evil age. Writers of apocalyptic literature claim to have received visions, dreams, or symbols from a heavenly intermediary who has given them a revelation of the future activity of God in history. The literary genre of Revelation, also known as the Apocalypse of John, is apocalyptic literature (not historical narrative) and should be imaginatively read as such. Reading and understanding the Apocalypse will not be an easy task, but it will be rewarding for all who have ears to hear its message. While the Apocalypse is not a clear and detailed map of the future, John does claim to receive revelation about the destiny of humanity and the world. His visions, images, and symbols need to be interpreted and decoded as we seek to live as God's people today.

The massive and important discussion of the relationship of apocalyptic to prophetic literature cannot be fully dealt with here, but it does need to be touched on as we begin. Prophecy can speak from the perspective of the present into the future, or speak to the present from the past. Usually, however, an apocalypse speaks from the perspective of the future into the present. The thought is that God will break into the present, but his action is pictured through the lens of a future time that will bring final judgement and renewal. Before delving into the Apocalypse, it is important for us to have several traits of apocalyptic literature in mind.

First, apocalyptic literature is dualistic in that there are two ages: the present evil age and the righteous age to come. God and Satan are in the battle of sovereignties. Satan is usually, although not in the Apocalypse of John, characterized as having control of the present evil age, while God is in control of the righteous age to come.

Second, it always speaks of a future time when God will break into history and bring an end to the present evil age. It is always eschatological, ultimately concerned with the end of the world.

Third, apocalyptic literature is pessimistic about the present age. All that matters is the future age of glory. There is more emphasis on awaiting the future than changing the present.

Fourth, it is usually pseudonymous; apocalyptic writers generally did not write in their own name but assigned their writings to a prominent figure from the past, a common practice in ancient times.

Fifth, apocalyptic literature uses symbols, images, and vision as the major vehicle for much of what it portrays.

The Apocalypse of John shares some of the above apocalyptic traits (the first, the second moderately, and the fifth). As essential as it is to realize that John's Apocalypse is similar in several ways to apocalyptic literature, it is equally important to focus on some distinctions.

The first distinction is that John is named as the author, serving as God's spokesman. The Apocalypse is not attributed to some prominent figure of the past, but gives John a present authority for writing. Second, the book is not only apocalyptic, but prophetic. The author is as concerned about living in the present as he is about the future. Third, John is positive about the present age as the age in which God is already victorious through the Lamb. The total defeat of Satan and evil eventually culminates in the new heavens and new earth. History is ultimately under the reign of God, not Satan, and the present age is not merely a parenthesis before the end, but the battlefield where God's redemptive acts take place. Furthermore, John is concerned with repentance and moral instruction for life now. Life now matters.

Now that we have noted several relations and distinctions between the Apocalypse of John and apocalyptic literature in general, it is important to be aware that there are at least four major ways the revelation of John has been interpreted:

(1) Preterist view—the book is read and understood only from a first century perspective; there is no prophecy for the future.
(2) Idealist view—throughout history God acts on basic principles expressed in the book.
(3) Historicist view—the book's interest lies solely in depicting historical events that are to unfold.
(4) Futurist view—there is a major emphasis on the future and the end times and little on the first century audience.

All four of these interpretive options contribute to our understanding of the Apocalypse. Readers should be careful not to merely choose one option and force the text to fit into its grid. A better understanding of the text comes about by attempting to maintain a certain degree of distance (already forced on the reader in the reading of any text) and to not have our minds made up before taking the necessary time to study the text.

The Apocalypse of John reveals a picture of the unfolding end of history, and we are given a glimpse behind its meaning and significance for both the present and the future. As we read and study the text it will become evident that the slain Lamb, who has purchased people for God, is victorious. He is standing.

All who are his share in this mighty victory, past, present, or future. They will be spared the wrath of God and experience direct community with him. God will wipe away every tear and the Lamb will be their shepherd, leading them to springs of living water. The consummation of God's reign is coming in a new heavens and earth. This gives us the context for the Apocalypse, for the whole of Scripture, and for the entirety of the lives we now live.

PROLOGUE (1:1-20)

INTRODUCTION TO THE APOCALYPSE

Text

(1-2) "The Apocalypse of Jesus Christ." The word *revelation* is *apokalypsis* in Greek. This word means 'an unfolding or unveiling of something hidden.' That is, a revealing of something that we could not discover for ourselves. Revelation is loaded and charged with perspectives that God graciously makes known, as opposed to knowledge uncovered by human wisdom or ingenuity.

Notice that the Apocalypse is mediated by Jesus Christ with the purpose of showing God's servants events that must shortly come to pass. We must remember that 'shortly' is used in a prophetic sense; the end therefore is always imminent. What God has planned for history *will* take place, but the aim of this unfolding is not so much chronology as it is hope and assurance.

John receives this revelation as testimony, which is vital to remember here, and also again when we come to the end of the book. To give testimony, in this context, is to faithfully witness to seeing revelation. God's ultimate plan has been revealed to John through an angel, although it is not always clear how readers are to understand 'angel.'

In the book of Revelation, angel usually means heavenly being or agent; however, the word can also mean human messenger. Other times the term angel may specifically and symbolically signify a Christ-like figure. For example, in 7:2 an angel comes from the East as the Messiah of Jewish expectation was predicted to do. This angel has the seal of God with which to seal his servants (the seal in the New Testament is primarily the Holy Spirit as seen in Eph. 1:13, 4:30). In 8:3 an angel is an intercessor for the saints. In 10:1 an angel is robed in a cloud (see also 1:7, 14:14-16). In 18:1 an angel has great authority and illumines the earth, and in 20:1 an angel holds the key to the Abyss, seizes Satan, and binds him (see also 1:18).

There are numerous occasions in the Old Testament where the same pattern is evident; Genesis Cf. 18:1 (9a, b), Cf. 19:1 (18, 20-21) and Judges Cf. 6:11 (14) are passages where God and his agent are related, though conceived as distinct. In each case, we must be attentive to the context and allow it to determine the meaning for us.

(3) Those who read, hear, and take to heart this prophecy from God are to be considered fortunate. In John's time a reading in church is the most likely scenario for the dissemination of this prophetic message, and perhaps this is something we should do more of today.

First, read, then listen, and finally obey.

This prophecy is not solely one of prediction, but also contains blessing, exhortation, and moral overtones which are to be acted upon.

Notice that this verse is the first of seven blessings or beatitudes in

Revelation (14:13, 16:15, 19:9, 20:6, 22:7, 14). We would do well to keep these in mind as they will have significant and profound theological and practical implications for the people of God and their salvation at crucial places throughout the book.

Greetings & Doxology (1:4-8)

The Apocalypse is written in the form of a letter or epistle, beginning with a standard greeting. It is addressed to the seven churches in Asia, but John was likely to have had a wider audience in mind when it was written. We want to be aware of the writer's two-fold concern: these original seven churches and ultimately all churches. Think of these early churches as symbolic for churches throughout the centuries. An immediate question arises.

Why did John select these seven churches? It is probable that the seven cities surrounding these churches were centers of communication where there had already been missional activity. For an itinerant Christian messenger the first city addressed, Ephesus, would have been a natural port of entry to mainland Asia. The other cities form a circular route around its inner territories.

(4-6) In regards to authorship, the author simply writes that he is John. No doubt his intimate knowledge of these seven churches and their knowledge of his authority were sufficient to make any further identification unnecessary. The letter begins as John's readers are greeted with grace and peace from God the Father. God is characterized as the one who was, is, and is to come. The author strategically aims to affirm God's consistency from age to age and to remind his audience that God is not constrained by time, but is sovereign over it.

Following the greeting, John refers to seven spirits. The reference occurs three times in this book (3:1, 4:5, 5:6), but nowhere else in the Scriptures or Jewish writings. Many take the seven spirits to be to angels. However, this seems unsatisfactory as the word is *spirits*, not angels or messengers. Usually the context provides clarification, so let's explore this further.

If we fast forward for a moment and look at 4:5 and 5:6, we can see the background for the symbolism of the seven spirits is found in Zech. 4:1-10. John may have incorporated the idea of lamps and eyes from this passage. Having the visions in 4:1-5:14 in mind, he then reproduces the same imagery here referring to the Holy Spirit. If this suggestion is appropriate, it is possible to press the connection between these visions of the seven spirits and the greeting a bit further. In 4:8 there is a proclamation of the Father's everlasting nature, holiness, and almighty power, which is echoed in this greeting in verse 4. In 5:9 the Lamb is proclaimed as King and Savior and by his death and resurrection his people are redeemed. This is echoed in verses 5-6.

It seems likely then that the author has shifted from the visions of the spirits in 4:1-5:14 (with their Zech. background) to his usage. Here, the seven spirits symbolize the Holy Spirit, perhaps in the Prologue intending to give a broader view of the Holy Spirit's work and function throughout the earth.

The testimony of the Holy Spirit's work as trustworthy reminds us that Jesus Christ is the 'faithful witness,' 'the firstborn from the dead,' and 'the ruler of kings and the earth,' mediating not only the Apocalypse, but also taking the role of a witness to truth from God. His testimony stands firm and he never compromises this truth. Those who read the Apocalypse are encouraged several times to follow Jesus' example of faithfulness.

As well as being described as a faithful witness, Jesus is the firstborn from the dead. This reference is an assurance that others will follow him; because of his resurrection and victory over death, he is firstborn of a new humanity and the one who reveals and redeems so that death no longer reigns.

Jesus is also the ruler of kings of the earth. He is King of Kings and will eventually be acknowledged by all as such. These verses, and those like them in the Apocalypse, played an important role in encouraging and assuring believers in John's time, who faced terrible persecution for having faith in Christ.

This confidence in Christ motivates John to break out into a doxology. Jesus loves us and has liberated Christians from sin by his precious and uniquely exquisite blood. Followed by an allusion to the Exodus (Ex. 19:5-6), which is again mentioned in 5:9, believers have been made a kingdom and priests, no doubt in subversive defiance of their persecutors, and are now connected with Christ. They are to serve his God and Father. As a result of this, John cannot help but praise the Son of God; to Christ be glory and power forever and ever!

(7) John's doxology brings us to a prophetic promise of the return of Christ, using the backdrop of both Dan. 7:13 and Zech. 12:10. Our understanding of this verse should derive from the context of the second coming of Christ. Because of this, all the peoples or tribes of the earth will mourn as judgement arrives. Christ's return is inevitable and with it will come God's final judgement. John emphasizes the gravity of this return by using both a Greek and Hebrew form of affirmation and approval: "So it is to be." "Amen."

(8) Using the Greek alphabet, God now refers to himself with the first and last letters. He is the beginning and the end. No power is greater than his. In spite of the difficult circumstances and devastating persecution, the Almighty himself professes his ultimate reign over the end of history. This magnificent and reassuring title, Alpha and Omega, occurs ten times in the New Testament, four of which are in the Apocalypse. We are meant to be attuned to the truth that God is reigning.

First Vision (1:9-20)

In these verses we are given a bit more information about the author, his commission to write, and his initial vision. John had probably been exiled to Patmos because of preaching the word of God and his faithful testimony to Jesus. As a result, he finds himself in a position similar to the churches he was writing.

(9) John refers to himself as both brother and companion in the suffering, the kingdom, and the patient endurance that believers have together in Jesus. This is a call to his readers to be strong and patient in the midst of present suffering. At the same time, he assures them that together they participate in the kingdom, God's messianic rule and all that this implies for believers. These three realities are the result of following Jesus. We all, at one point or another, go through times of suffering and John calls us to do so with fortitude and patience. There must be a willingness to suffer with Christ if one is going to access the promise to reign with him.

(10a) "On the Lord's day" John was "in the Spirit." In this instance, 'the Lord's day' is probably a reference to the first day of the week. Let's develop this phrase in more detail before we go any further.

We need to begin by asking a couple of questions. Does the phrase, 'on the Lord's day' have anything to say to us today? Should 'the Lord's day,' which was intimately connected with the first day of the week, also the day of Christ's resurrection, be considered normative for worship? Some regard it as such. However, those that do also maintain there is no biblical principle for this; it is only the tradition of the church. Is this tradition sufficient? Those who argue for normativity argue for the right thing but on the wrong basis. Tradition, it is argued, is to be followed for tradition's sake.

Others see the Reformers as having the right view of this phrase. Both Calvin and Luther, among others at this time, saw first-day worship 'on the Lord's day' as just a convenient institution, useful for the practical ordering of church life. Remember, the Reformers were concerned to affirm *sola scriptura*, Scripture alone. For them, canonical status for a particular practice was primary. If this was lacking, one could not consider such a practice normative. For the Reformers there is no biblical principle involved with 'the Lord's day.'

To a degree, this is fair enough. We should applaud the Reformers' efforts to emphasize *Scripture* alone. It is not tradition which gives us Scripture, but Scripture which gives us tradition (even though we could say there is something of a mixing of these in the sense of oral tradition, the preaching of the Gospel, etc. at certain stages of the historical development of the canon). Nonetheless, the concept that tradition derives from Scripture and should always be critiqued by Scripture demands priority.

However, having affirmed the efforts of the Reformers and their emphasis on *sola scriptura*, I would nevertheless disagree with their conclusions regarding 'the Lord's day' being merely a convenient institution. It seems they may have neglected to look closely at Revelation 1:10. Our text says 'on the Lord's day.' This appears to be a title for a day that carried with it more significance than another. If this is so, this verse provides a critique of both the Traditionalists and the Reformers. While it is certainly true that every day is the Lord's, this particular text references one particular day. At this point, another question arises. If every day is the Lord's, why was there a specific 'Lord's day'?

The practice of gathered worship on this day was based on Christ's resurrection, affirming his lordship not just over the church, but over history and the cosmos as well. Every day is the Lord's because there is one specific 'Lord's day' and not the other way around. To reverse this is to have misunderstood the profound effect of the resurrection. Because of *this* day, the day we now celebrate, we can say each day is the Lord's.

A body of believers meeting on Sunday morning stands in the stream of believing Christians throughout the generations who have gathered together especially 'on the Lord's day.' This is to remind each other and the watching world of Christ's finished work on the cross and his victory over death in the resurrection. We meet and celebrate together not because of *tradition*, nor because of *convenience*, but because of the resurrection.

Certainly when we as believers do meet we are to encourage each other as best we can, but this is not the primary reason for us coming together. We gather because there is something to encourage each other about; God is there and Christ is raised. The Lamb who took away the sins of the world is victorious and will someday return consummating the rule he inaugurated with his first coming. We don't meet together primarily for encouragement's sake, neither do we meet together solely for worship's sake. Worship is not the context for worship. Encouragement is not the context for encouragement. These are insufficient reasons for coming together.

Worship and encouragement are contextual in the sense that they emerge from something much larger. God's existence, Christ's redemptive work, God's acts in history, past, present, and future in the power of the Spirit are revealed to us in Scripture, the living Word of God, which is sharper than a two-edged sword, piercing to the bone and marrow. This gives us the context for worship and encouragement. Worship is the community's *recognition* of its Lord, not its creator. Worship is not an escape. On the contrary, it firmly entrenches us in the battle of sovereignties in that we, through meeting together, are a sign of the reality that Christ is victorious over evil and death.

Worship is a central motif in the Apocalypse. Consider the hymns of worship to God and to the Lamb found in 4:1-5:14. In 13:8 there is also worship, but this time of the beast. Those who worship the Lamb are in direct conflict with those who worship something else. The victory of the Lamb and the subsequent worship that stems from it engages us in the battle of the Apocalypse. In our worship 'on the Lord's day' we already express Christ's lordship as it is now and will be forever and ever. The Lord's day is an eschatological day. Christians meet today because of an eschatological basis rooted in the historical resurrection of Christ and the future consummation of the rule of God.

It must be said that John's objective is not to teach us something about a day of worship; however, his reference does show us that a New Testament pattern was already established and in practice at his time of writing. The significance of the phrase 'on the Lord's day' is not that it establishes a pattern, but that it affirms that one already exists. As far as I'm concerned, this pattern is to be followed and for good reason. Our meeting is rooted in the resurrection itself. This should be a living reality which brings about a desire to worship together. It is not legalistic. To meet together is to celebrate the historical resurrection of Christ and its present and future meaning for each of us, the world in which we live, indeed, the entire cosmos.

On the Lord's day, John was 'in the Spirit.' The reference to John's being in the Spirit infers that he was in a trance-like state that was simply not the norm for all Christians. The vision comes to him in Spirit, suggesting it is not of his own making, invention, or formulation. It is noteworthy that John does not put tremendous value on the experience per se. He does not discuss the 'how' of his condition, but rather seems to emphasize the revelation itself and its inspiration. The experience is not a normal everyday occurrence, but due to the special intervention of the Spirit.

(10b-11) John hears a loud voice like a trumpet. Trumpets are associated with theophanies—visions in the Old Testament of God (Ex. 19:16) and are also the instrument used to announce the coming of Christ in the New Testament (1 Cor. 15:52). The voice commands John to write and transmit the Apocalypse to the seven churches.

(12-14) John turns to see who is speaking to him and sees the seven golden lampstands, which symbolize the seven churches. Among the lampstands is One like a son of man (Dan. 7:9ff). This reference to the son of man is instructive for identifying the speaker as Jesus himself used the phrase in regard to his own mission and ministry. John describes him as wearing a long robe with a golden sash (Dan. 10:4ff), something only a person of great distinction would wear. His head and hair were white like wool or snow. The description here picks up and uses the same type of language used in Daniel for the Ancient of Days. "His eyes were like blazing fire" may be adapted from Daniel 10:6.

(15-16) "His feet were like bronze and his voice like the sound of rushing waters" denote both strength and stability. "In his right hand he held the seven stars and out of his mouth came a sharp two-edged sword." The seven stars are the angels of the seven churches and the sword refers to divine judgement. "His face was brilliant as the sun" (verse 16). This reminds us of the transfiguration in Matthew 17 where Jesus' face shone like the sun.

(17-20) John falls "as though dead" at the feet of the one he has seen. This is a typical reaction, often found in association with theophanies. Daniel 10:8ff may provide some background. The same right hand that holds the seven stars is placed on John. Again, note the author's intent is not so much to reconstruct how Christ can hold the seven stars and touch him, but rather to signify that the One who touched him is the One who has the power to hold the churches secure, while also consoling and commissioning him.

The prophet is not to fear in the midst of this magnificent vision. The one he sees, the one speaking and the one who touched him is the 'First and the Last.' The 'First and the Last' corresponds to the 'Alpha and Omega' of 1:8 and is without question a title of divinity, both here and in the Old Testament. The 'First and the Last' is the 'Living One.' He who was dead is now alive forever and ever. He died at a particular point in history, but since the resurrection on Easter Sunday he lives forever. The crucified and risen One brought about the new exodus, solving both the problem of Israel's failure to be a light to the nations and our bondage to sin and death, by opening the way to redeemed life. He also holds the keys to death and Hades and has victory over them. Even death itself could not stop the dynamic power of the Gospel.

The vision John sees is clearly of the risen and glorified Christ. He is the Lamb of God, the Living One, the First and the Last. The One who is seen among the seven lampstands and holds the seven stars in his right hand is the crucified and risen One who assures the churches of both his presence with them and his power to sustain them through any and every persecution. This is the same One to whom many of the metaphors referring explicitly to God in the Old Testament are now applied. He is the very same One who loves us and has liberated us and made us to be a kingdom of priests (1:5-6). He is also the One who commands John to write what he has seen including what is now and what will take place later.

Some interpreters argue that what John has seen refers to the vision of Christ in 1:9-20; while what is now relates to the present condition of the seven churches as expressed in the seven letters (2:1-3:22); and what will take place later concerns the future contained in the rest of the book. While this division is helpful in one sense, there are several problems with its trajectory.

What I have in mind is this: chapters 4:1-22:21 do not refer *exclusively* to the future. Sometimes the past or the present is also in view. No doubt these chapters do refer to the future, but the problem lies with thinking that this is their only concern. Another problem of the same order exists with the seven letters to the seven churches. To categorize these letters as only referring to the 'now' is not entirely wrong; it is helpful to a point. However, these letters are not exclusively concerned with the present condition of these particular churches. Future concerns are also integrated and addressed.

Let us keep in mind that past, present, and future are woven together throughout the whole Apocalypse. Certainly the thrust is orientated toward the future, but this does not permit us to downplay or isolate various frameworks of time, unless the text itself gives a clear indication that we should do so.

In verse 20, we come to the conclusion of chapter 1. John is given the explanation of the mystery of the seven stars and the seven lampstands. The seven stars are the angels of the seven churches and the seven lampstands are the seven churches. Despite this new information, the symbolic imagery remains complex and difficult to decode.

THE SEVEN LETTERS (2:1-3:22)

General Review

The opening of the Apocalypse has provided us with a magnificent proclamation of blessing to those who read and obey what is testified to and written. John's prophetic address is to the seven churches in Asia, but equally, in a symbolic manner, to all churches. Grace and peace from God, who was, is, and is to come and Jesus Christ, who has provided redemption and made his followers into a subversive kingdom serving God.

We also developed, more extensively, verse 10 and the phrase 'on the Lord's Day.' I suggested, against both the traditional and reformation views that we meet together not because of tradition, nor because of social convenience, nor for the practical ordering of the life of the church. The real reason we meet for worship is because of the resurrection of Christ. This is 'the Lord's Day.'

Attention was also given to the notion of John's being 'in the Spirit' and the reception of the command to write to the seven churches (see 1:9-20, John's first vision). In verse 12 John turns to 'see,' implying here the visionary aspect of what he is now about to describe. We concluded that this majestic vision was of the crucified, risen, and glorified Christ. Many of the Old Testament metaphors that describe God, especially from the book of Daniel, are now used by John in his description of the 'one like a son of man.'

In verses 17-18 the prophet falls at the feet of Christ as though dead, but is told not to fear. The one he sees is the First and the Last—the Living One—the One who was dead, but who now lives forever and ever.

Verse 19 includes the command to write what was seen, what is now, and what will take place later. These are not to be taken as statements of time that provide neat divisions of the book, for past, present, and future concerns are woven in and through all parts of the Apocalypse.

In verse 20 we were given the explanation of the mystery of the seven stars in Christ's right hand and of the seven golden lampstands among which he is seen (see 1:13, 16). The seven stars are the angels of the churches and the seven lampstands are the churches.

This brief review of chapter 1 leads us into some preliminary considerations on the seven letters—proclamations in chapters 2-3 that are addressed "to 'the angel' of the church in..." We may quickly find ourselves dissatisfied with the previous explanation of the seven stars being the angels of the seven churches. What does this mean? Why are all the letters addressed to an 'angel'? Or are we to think that the churches had some sort of guardian angel? Were these letters addressed to human messengers or leaders, perhaps something like bishops in the churches? Let's explore these questions in further detail.

Many today put forward the latter suggestion, however, it may not be the most accurate. While it is true that the word 'angel' almost always means messenger and is found over sixty times in the Apocalypse, not including these letters, it is noteworthy that each of these times it refers to a heavenly being. Consequently, it seems unlikely that the address to 'angel' in the letters is a reference to a human messenger or leader.

What about the possibility that these angels are guardian angels? While uncommon, this view is not completely without merit. There is a reference to this in the book of Daniel (10:13, 20, 21), where nations seem to have something like a guardian angel. In our context however, this is difficult to support as it does not quite make sense to see John as commissioned to write these letters to guardian angels with instructions for them to perform their guardianship more effectively. A further problem with this interpretation, as well as the previous one, lies within the letters themselves. Each of them has the particular congregations and specific location in mind, and is practically concerned with their daily lives.

Another interpretation considers the angels as heavenly counterparts of earthly congregations. This should not be taken literally, as if John sees the congregations seated in the heavens above, answering to their equivalents below. It is better to think of them as existentially in heaven though living on earth. In other words, we can imagine this as symbolically conveying the truth that there is an aspect of heavenly existence related to their earthly lives in Christ.

John writes to earthly communities characterized by their failures and weaknesses, successes and strengths. However, these communities have one feature which distinguishes them from any other earthly communities. They are said to be 'in Jesus' and are therefore made priests and a kingdom with him (1:6, 9). It is because of this fact that John addresses his letters to the 'angel'. He is aiming to show these Christians that they have a heavenly orientation as their existence is also 'in Jesus' who is in heaven. Their earthly conduct and actions should reflect this heavenly existence and it is this existence that John wants to stress. Of course, we must remember that Christ is also in the midst of the lampstands. These two realities, Christ present with the church on earth and they with him in heaven are cause for great reassurance, especially in the midst of terrible persecution.

It may be helpful here to think of the two images used in 1:20. We have stars (angels) and lampstands, both of which seem to point to the churches and both of which symbolize light. One is an earthly light, the other heavenly. Is it possible that this reflects the dual character of the church? If so, perhaps the two-sided nature of the church works out something like this: First, the church must act to preserve faith in Christ in the face of persecution and hardship. The church is to keep its lampstand lit as the turbulent winds of deceit seek to extinguish the light of the gospel. The assurance that this can be carried out and the protection it offers comes from the fact that Christ is among the lampstands (1:13).

Second, the churches were, as the church is today, an eschatological reality. They and we already belong, in some sense, to the new world. Each individual who has believed on Christ is made a new creation. That new creation is in reality a *sign* of the rule of God breaking into the world (first through the coming of Christ, then through the very existence of the church as we who are part of it await the redemption of our bodies and the universe itself upon Christ's return), and transferring us from one rule to the other. In other words, the future has broken into the present. Therefore, those in Christ already share and participate in the reality of being present with God in heaven just as the stars and angels. The assurance of this reality and the protection it offers is found in the fact that Christ holds the seven stars (angels) in his right hand. This indicates his power to sustain the churches through any and every persecution or difficulty (see Eph. 2:6-10; Phil. 3:15-21; and Col. 3:1 for Paul's view of this interpretive option where he clearly emphasizes the 'already but not yet' feature of salvation).

In all seven letters there is a clear indication that the speaker is Christ, and a careful look shows us that each letter echoes back to chapter 1 (2:1 corresponds to 1:12-15, 2:8 and 1:17-18, 2:12 and 1:16, 2:18 and 1:14-15, 3:1 and 1:4, 16, 3:7 and 1:18, 3:14 and 1:2).

There is then a remarkably close relationship between the letters and chapter 1. We also should keep in mind, however, that the relationship of the letters to other parts of the book is pertinent as well. The heavenly city of Jerusalem in chapters 21 and 22 is contrasted to the seven earthly cities in that it is God's city, the city to which all the promises made to the earthly cities looks forward. In chapters 4-20 there are also parallels of expression or symbol, suggesting John may have had the circumstances of the churches in mind, calling for patient endurance and faithfulness, giving warnings against idolatry, and Satan's powerful and attractive deceptions.

The point we need to continue to focus on is that there is an internal coherence to the book as different parts relate to each other. Going further, we could also say there is an overall coherence between the Apocalypse and the rest of Scripture. Systematic and precise divisions fail to do justice to the text.

These letters, as the rest of the Apocalypse, are as pertinent today as they ever were. Think of the churches as symbolic for churches throughout the centuries. Consider the impoverished state of the church in our times. Consumerism, idolatry, confused and superficial theology and spirituality, empty minds and blinded hearts, characterize far too many Christians and churches, showing that we have much to learn from each letter. Read together they will provide critique, wisdom and insight for our lives. As we face the powerful threat of cultural, religious and political manifestations that set themselves up as authoritative and endanger faith and allegiance to the crucified and risen One, we want to be informed about and aware of whom we follow and obey.

The Letter to Ephesus (2:1-7)

Introduction

Ephesus was one of the prominent cities of the ancient world and may have even been the greatest in all of Asia Minor. The famous temple of Artemis was located there, as well as two temples devoted to emperor worship (see Acts 19:17-41). Religious syncretism proliferated and there was much superstition. No doubt this strongly pagan environment contributed to making life difficult for Christians, much as it does for us in our Ephesus today.

Text

(1) The letter, as we have seen, is addressed to "the angel of the church in Ephesus." Clearly, the prophetic message is for the church itself. The words about to be spoken are those of the "one like a son of man," the same one who has been identified with similar characteristics as the Ancient of Days. He is the risen Christ who is present in the midst of the churches.

The formulaic introduction, "these are the words," found in all the letters is very close to the prophetic pronouncement in the Old Testament ("thus says the Lord") and not only reminds us of the prophetic character of these seven letters, but also of the whole of the Apocalypse. Each letter concludes with a formulaic exhortation: "Let anyone who has an ear listen to what the Spirit says to the churches."

(2-3) We have a recurring affirmation (see the other six letters) of the exalted Christ's knowledge of what is going on among his people, one of the most important motifs in each letter and especially applicable to us today. Christ is with his people. He knows what's happening in their midst, both corporately and individually. He knows their deeds; he knows of their hard work and perseverance to hold on to true faith in him.

In addition, the passage compliments the Christians in Ephesus for their steadfastness in difficult times. These are all characteristics of the Christian life—there are certainly others, but in this context these are emphasized. Christians at Ephesus had succeeded in not accepting evil men and in testing those who claimed to be apostles, but were charlatans. It is a pity we are not as careful today.

(4) The Ephesians are charged nevertheless, with forsaking their "first love." 'First love' in this context primarily refers to a love for one another. However, this lack of love for one another may be rooted in a loss of love for God. Perhaps, the Christians in Ephesus overemphasized good works and some non-essentials of God's redemption in Christ, thereby creating an atmosphere of back-biting and suspicion in which their love for one another could no longer be practiced. They may have fallen into some form of dogmatic orthodoxy, which helped them in regard to not tolerating the evil men and false apostles, but it left no room for Jesus' teaching in John 13:35, "by this all people will know that you are my disciples, if you have love for one another." Without this others-directed love, what they supposed was orthodoxy fell far short of its goal.

(5) Christ exhorts the believers to first of all 'remember' where they used to be. In other words, 'You used to love one another and God, but now you've created a situation where neither can take place.'

We too should consider this: how often do we set up situations and atmospheres where it is next to impossible to love God and one another? Whether it is personal issues related to pride, arrogance, or some other manifestation of sin, there is a call to focus on redemption and learn in a deeper way the meaning and relevance of Christ's salvific work. A redeemed memory is crucial to living out our faith for the sake of Christ and for others. How important it is to remember well!

The second exhortation is to repent. This motif surfaces again and again in the letters. Notice carefully the directive is not just repent, but repent and do the things you did at first. The church is called to action. If there is no repentance the church will be removed from its place with Christ and the other lampstands. The danger of immediate judgement is stressed, but at this point it is not yet a certainty. Repent and do are crucial imperatives for this church to embody. The possibility of the church regaining its 'first love' is very real, though this can only be recovered by remembering, repenting, and doing.

(6) Verse 5 is followed by a commendation for hating the practices of the Nicolaitans, just as Christ does. The Nicolaitans were most likely a libertarian sect who compromised with the pagan society around them. This gives us another indication of the high level of syncretism at Ephesus and the pressure the Christians there faced.

(7) This is an exhortation to hear what the Spirit says to the churches, but it is Christ who is speaking. The verse seems to imply the word of Christ is the word of the Spirit. Christ is not identical with the Spirit, but he speaks to the churches through the Spirit. The relation between the two here is very similar to that in John 16:12-15.

The next phrase, "to everyone who conquers," should not fix our attention solely on the individual overcomer, but on Christ himself who through his sacrifice makes the victory possible. His victory gives the believer the potential to persist in faith and persevere in hope to the end. All who overcome are granted the "right to eat of from the tree of life" (representing everlasting life and renewal in this context). "Let anyone who has an ear listen to what the Spirit says to the churches."

Summary

We examined the first of the seven letters to the churches in 2:1-7 and noted the reference back to the risen and glorified Christ in verse 1. He is the speaker as well as the One who knows their deeds. They have persevered and endured hardships for his name and have not grown weary.

Yet in verse 4 they are said to have lost their 'first love.' The most probable explanation of this was the church's loss of love for one another, possibly growing out of a lack of love for God. The Christians in Ephesus are called to first to remember, then to repent, and finally to do what they had previously done. In their favor was the fact that they, as Christ, hated the practices of the Nicolaitans, practices probably involving some form of pagan worship.

In verse 7 we then were reminded, as we are in all the letters, to hear what the Spirit says to the churches. The one who overcomes can do so only because Christ has already overcome.

The Letter to Smyrna (2:8-11)

Introduction

Smyrna was a large city with a passionate loyalty to Rome. There were temples erected to the goddess of Rome and to many Roman leaders. Christians in Smyrna were surrounded by this pagan environment and challenged to live in allegiance to the crucified and risen One. This is both a joy and a task. We may find ourselves in quite similar situations, needing insightful guidance and true wisdom in following in the footsteps of Christ.

Text

(8) "These are the words" is an affirmation of the prophetic character of what is to follow. The identification of the speaker as the First and the Last, the One who died and has come to life, refers back to 1:17-18. There is again in this letter the explicit relationship of the risen Christ to the church. To those facing persecution, even death, he is the victor and is in their midst.

(9) Christ knows their difficulties. He is aware of their poverty, which may have been brought about by the confiscation of their goods and property. Even in the midst of these problems he says, "You are rich." This is likely to be a reference to their spiritual richness. We can contrast this with the letter to Laodicea (3:17-18):

> You say, 'I am rich; I have acquired wealth and do not need a thing.' But you do not realize that you are wretched, pitiful, poor, blind, and naked. I counsel you to buy from me gold refined in the fire, so that you can become rich; white clothes to wear, so you can cover your nakedness...

This is such a good lesson for us to hear. Similar to the Laodiceans, we often equate material possessions with riches. It would seem, on the contrary, that true riches are spiritual. In 3:18 one is counseled to buy from Christ gold refined in the fire, the true way to become rich. Purity comes from Christ alone.

The thought here stands against much of what we are bombarded with in our own day concerning values and wealth. We can say there are two senses of being rich and two senses of being poor. In each case both are dependent on one's relationship to Christ. Consider and ponder these important words for yourself and the church today!

The next part of the verse shows that the Jews themselves were likely to have been involved in the persecution of Christians at Smyrna. In this case the persecutors may have been Jews according to the flesh, since in the New Testament a true Jew is one who is in Christ (Rom. 2:28-29).

These persecutors of the Smyrnian Christians were not really Jews in this sense. They had in fact degenerated into becoming Satan's advocates (see John 8:42-47). The 'synagogue of Satan' may refer to a specific Jewish synagogue in the city where there was a particular anti-Christian attitude resulting in persecution of the Christian community.

(10) It is worth noting again the motif running through the book that things may get even worse, but believers are not to fear. Even though persecution takes place through the Jews, Roman authorities, or others, it is ultimately the devil that is at the root of the problem. This motif comes to its summit in 17:1-18:24 where we find the judgement on Babylon. Deception and evil continue until the ultimate defeat of the devil himself in 20:1-15.

It is important to remember in the Apocalypse and in some sense throughout Scripture that there is this conflict between sovereignties, which in this book is clearly resolved with God as victor (also Eph. 6:10-18). Some of the believers will therefore suffer and be put into prison for an indefinite period of time. The devil will put them to the test. For some this may ultimately result in death for their faith and believers are called to be faithful even in the midst of horrendous circumstances. They are encouraged not to give up. The Lamb is, and will be, victorious.

This is another vital lesson for us. In the midst of trials and tribulations one is to hold on to life, not death. I would suggest that there may be some confusion for us here as many of us may be in the habit of embracing death rather than life. We are attracted to false apostles, chase after idols, and are enamoured with material possessions. The call is to be faithful. But to what? To God, to Christ and his redeeming work, and to the ultimate difference that work makes to the orientation or goal of one's life. This should be a powerful reality in our lives. If it is not, we should be asking ourselves some serious questions. Do we really believe, and if so are we choosing and acting in accord with our belief? What a tremendous challenge for the church. Choosing and acting on God's revelation means far more than just talking about it. Faith is an action and a choice that has an impact on the world for the sake of Christ and his redemption.

Maybe we need to be in the position of suffering persecution for there to be that 'cutting edge' necessity of holding firm to the faith. Do we have it too easy? By this I don't mean to downplay the seriousness of our own struggles, but only to say that in whatever the circumstances, we are called to choose life and to act upon it. We must affirm this reality through our choices and actions and work out our salvation for God is at work in us (Phil. 3:12-21).

(11) We again have the formulaic closing of the promise to the one who remains faithful and overcomes. This one will not be hurt by the second death, which in the Apocalypse is seen as final destruction, whereas the first death is merely physical. The relevance of this verse, for both the Christians at Smyrna and for us, is clear.

In some cases there will be periods of trial, even to the extent of death. Death at the hands of others is a travesty, but ultimately irrelevant when compared with the awesome judgement of God. Everyone who overcomes persecution will receive the crown of life, emphatically contrasted here with the destiny of the second death. Both are real prospects; therefore, those who already possess life must take care to hold on to it in all circumstances as they look forward to receiving the crown. In this way the faithful will avoid God's punishment and therefore live forever in his presence. "Let anyone who has an ear listen to what the Spirit says to the churches."

The Letter to Pergamum (2:12-17)

Introduction

Pergamum was not a city noted for its commerce, but for its great library and its importance as a center for many different forms of religious activity. In this regard, the imperial cult (emperor worship) was prominent, though not exclusive. The pagan god Asclepis was well known here and many came to the city to be healed. Temples to Zeus were in operation and several temples devoted to emperor worship existed. Living in Pergamum, surrounded by this deceptive religious environment, Christians were facing serious challenges to their faith.

Text

(12) The familiar phrase 'these are the words' affirms the prophetic announcement. This time it is made by the One with the sharp two-edged sword. The reference goes back to 1:16 and confirms that Christ is the speaker.

(13) Christ's words "I know where you live," shows us his personal knowledge of their situation. He is in their midst. The reference to "where Satan has his throne" may be tied in with the fact that city of Pergamum was the center of the imperial cult, which propagated emperor worship. In these overwhelmingly pagan conditions the Christians had remained faithful. This portrayal suggests that difficulties in maintaining their faith had been experienced. No doubt, as mentioned, this involved the martyrdom of Antipas, a faithful witness to Christ.

(14-15) Christ has a few things against the church. Some in their midst hold to the teachings of Balaam, probably a typological reference, which represents incorrect and misleading teaching. Such a false perspective manifests itself through the Nicolaitans. As Balaam had misled the Israelites in the Old Testament resulting in their apostasy through idolatry and immorality (Num. 25:1, 31:16), so now the Nicolaitans were doing the same kind of thing in the midst of the church. They seem to be an enemy from within. The Nicolaitans' standard is one of compromise with their pagan environment. Perhaps, they were saying, 'Oh yes, faith in Christ is important, but it is not important enough to be persecuted for. It really doesn't matter if one compromises and worships the emperor and is involved in all sorts of pagan activity.' Compromise, not confrontation, was the way to survive. Where are we today? Lamentably, notions of compromise proliferate in the church, while confrontation is rare.

There is a fine line here between legalism and liberty. Where are we to confront, rather than compromise with our surroundings and contemporary lifestyle? How far do we go in the pursuit of personal peace and affluence, versus deciding what is right and wrong? Take the examples of divorce and prosperity. Sadly, the rate of divorce in the church today is almost as high as outside it. In many cases this is a result of compromise, often for nothing more than convenience or the fulfilment of immoral desires on the part of men and women. And prosperity has become the bane of the church. When riches are more important than people we've lost our way. Christians must stand together in confrontation, not compromise! Graciously challenging our culture and the church that follows it for the sake of Christ, is one of our vital callings.

(16) In addition, the whole church is to repent. What a revolutionary idea. Imagine the whole church in a city or country today recognizing the need to repent and begin anew. This could start with a mass public confession that we have sinned and not loved as we should. God forgive us and bring us a new beginning.

The church's integrity and credibility in Pergamum is severely threatened. Some have accommodated to immorality and idolatry and must become more like the church at Ephesus in their testing of false apostles and their unwillingness to tolerate such compromise (see 2:2). A failure to repent will result in Christ coming in judgement, both to the church and those responsible for the things taking place.

(17) The conclusion incorporates two promises to the faithful. First, the hidden manna may allude to the tradition of the manna hidden by Jeremiah at the time of the destruction of the temple. There was a golden pot of manna kept in the temple (see Ex. 16:32-34; Heb. 9:4), and when the temple disappeared it was thought that this would re-appear with the arrival of the Messiah.

It is probably fair to see the manna as a reference to everlasting life, much as the tree of life was in the letter to Ephesus. Perhaps, the image refers to John 6:25-59. Here the manna is given in the desert, but it is not true bread. The fathers eat, but yet they die.

However, in Jesus, God gives true bread. If anyone eats of this bread they will live forever as Jesus is the living bread which came down from heaven (see Jn. 6:47-51, 58). There may also be a contrast here between the eating of food sacrificed to idols and being given hidden manna to eat. Those who eat food sacrificed to idols in this context are faced with the sword of Christ, while those who overcome are given everlasting life.

The second promise, 'a white stone with a new name on it known only to the receiver,' is more cryptic. Numerous interpretations for this are in play, but we will stay with those most relevant to the context, while at the same time acknowledging that it is impossible to be able to decode this symbolism with any certainty as to the text's meaning.

One possible interpretation is that the 'white stone' refers to a jury acquittal. In ancient times, a white stone was given to one who was innocent and a black stone was given to those found guilty. In this case, the white stone signifies the victor's acquittal on the day of judgement.

A different possibility considers the 'white stone' a ticket of admission to festivals or assemblies. This could relate to the messianic banquet and therefore be some sort of extension of the idea already found concerning the hidden manna.

On the other hand, some would see the reference to the 'new name' known only to the receiver as carrying the major emphasis. From a biblical point of view, 'name' may have to do with character. If this is the case, the new name refers to the quality, nature, or status of the receiver. In other words, the new name was a reference to the receiver's new character and known only to the receiver in the sense that one's reception of it is between he or she and God.

If this is so, the reception of this new character is and must be embraced and experienced by the one who overcomes. This means that no one can receive this reality and assurance for us, nor can we live on the basis of another's experiences. The reality of new life must be experienced now by each person as we look forward in hope to its final completion and our eventual and ultimate transformation on the glorious day when we are privileged to see Christ face to face. "Let anyone who has an ear listen to what the Spirit says to the churches."

Summary

We explored the second and third letters to the churches in 2:8-17. In both letters we noted the identification of Christ as the speaker, referring us back to chapter 1.

> The words are those of the First and the Last (2:8) and the One who has the sharp double edged sword (2:12).

In the letter to Smyrna, it was pointed out that in some sense they were poor—yet rich. They were, in fact, spiritually rich, though they suffered afflictions and were about to suffer even more. They were tested by the devil for a period of time, but in the midst of this they were called to be faithful, despite facing the ultimate and devastating consequence of death. Anyone who overcomes will not be harmed by the second death or the finality of death.

Four things stand out in this letter:

1) Christ is the speaker and has authority to speak as the First and the Last, as the One who died and came to life.
2) Christ knows the situation of the church at Smyrna. He recognizes their poverty but proclaims them to be rich.
3) Believers are being persecuted and will be tested by the devil.
4) Believers are called to be faithful in spite of this persecution, with the promise that the one who overcomes will not be hurt by the second death.

After Smyrna, the next letter is addressed to Pergamum. It is evident that this church is suffering persecution by an extremely pagan and hostile environment as well. In face of this persecution, they have not renounced Christ, but have remained true to his name and faithful to his authority.

In this letter, however, there are a few things stated against this church. There are some in their midst who hold to false teaching. The whole church is called to repent or face judgement.

Anyone who overcomes will be given the sustenance of hidden manna and a cryptic white stone with a new name.

Four things stand out in this letter:

1) Christ is the speaker and has the authority to speak as the One with the sharp double edged sword.
2) He knows their situation and that they have remained strong and not renounced their faith in spite of persecution stemming from their pagan surroundings.
3) They must purge the false teaching and are called to repent or face judgement.
4) The one who overcomes will be given everlasting life.

The Letter to Thyatira (2:18-29)

Introduction

Thyatira was the least known and least remarkable of all the cities in the letters. The city was rather plain, not having the visual splendor or character of the others. The words of the letter are addressed to a developing church in a growing city, neither of which had gained the prominence of Ephesus.

We learn from the ancient inscriptions that Thyatira was a manufacturing center comprising wool and garment workers, potters, dyers, tanners, and bronze smiths. From these inscriptions we also learn that trade guilds, or what we might today call trade unions, were set up for the craftspeople. These guilds played a major role in the life of the city.

Trade was so important to the Thyatirans that they even had their own god, Tyrimnos, who was a provider and advocate for the city trades. Some coins manufactured here had this god pictured on them. Tyrimnos is represented as grasping the emperor's hand, while other coins celebrate the deification of the emperor Domitian's son, portraying him seated on a globe surrounded by seven stars.

Because of such strong Roman influences, we again need to be aware of the activity of the imperial cult in this city. The Thyatiran Christians were exposed to an organized paganism which impinged on their lives in many ways.

John writes to assure them and to warn them about the dangers of succumbing to these influences. The words of the victorious Christ show he is the true patron of the church and its work. He is the 'Son of God' arrayed with notably very similar characteristics as the carefully refined metal produced in the furnaces of their city.

As we look at the letter in more detail, keep this introduction to the local context in mind as it will be helpful, even essential, to understanding the text. We will see that a raised awareness of environmental particulars provides a useful picture for relevant theological application that holds true for our own contexts and situations. Whenever we can have pertinent background information about a city, its people, and culture it will enhance and enrich our interpretation of the text.

Text

(18) The title, 'the Son of God' appears here for the first and only time in the Apocalypse. The Son of God stands in stark contrast to the local deities and the Roman emperor. He is the crucified and risen One, the true and only Son of God. The eyes of blazing fire and the feet of burnished bronze no doubt carry local significance for the Thyatirans and at the same time leave no question as to whose words these are. This same description is used by John as he turns to see who is speaking to him in the first vision (see 1:12-16).

(19-20) The risen Christ is not unaware of the deeds of the Thyatirans. John notes there is more love, faith, service, and perseverance than there was previously. (This church then stands in contrast to Ephesus where the believers are told to do the things they did at first). However, there are some problems with the church. The teaching of the prophetess Jezebel is misleading believers. Consequently, this false teaching is similar to that of the Nicolaitans in the letter to Pergamum.

Jezebel of the Old Testament is the link. It was she who enticed many Israelites to the cult of Baal (1 Kings 18:4, 19). The parallel is, as Jezebel in the Old Testament misled the Israelites, this Jezebel in Thyatira is doing the same thing in the midst of the church. Often in these letters the greatest threat to believers is the threat from within. The contrast between untruth and truth is subtle, yet profound. A half-truth is usually more deceptive than an outright lie. Therefore, in our own day, whether it's Greek philosophy, materialism, New Age, or some form of contemporary humanism, Christians must be aware that the threat is as real from inside as it is from outside the church.

(21) The woman representing Jezebel is a destructive influence who refuses to repent, implying that the prophetess has already been warned. She has been given time, but she has refused.

(22-23a) The result of the refusal to repent is impending judgement. She will be inflicted with suffering and her followers will suffer great tribulation unless they repent, literally, of her works. Her children will be killed, putting an end to her misleading seduction into a compromised Christianity.

Certainly, the Christians of Thyatira were in a difficult place. As I mentioned earlier, the trade unions were likely to have been a focal part of local life. There is some evidence for feasts or assemblies taking place in the city. These types of functions were probably where the pressure was put on to conform to various forms of idolatry or sexual immorality. I imagine many fraternities or organizations today are similar. Because of business reasons, if being a member of the 'right' organization is advantageous, many Christians might think, "Why not? It's not really idolatrous or immoral to be involved in various initiation rites and besides, being a member of that social group is good for business." We must be careful here not to compromise. Idolatry is a serious, although a not always evident, matter.

(23b) The judgement over Thyatira in verses 22-23a will not go unnoticed. All the churches will realize that it is Christ who searches the inner being and it is he who will give to each one according to his or her deeds (Jas. 2:14 ff; Rom. 2:3 ff).

(24-25) Christ now addresses those who have not compromised. No other burden will be placed on them. They are to hold onto what they have, a reference most likely to verse 19, until Christ's return.

(26-29) Two things are to be given to those who overcome and do the works of Christ, as contrasted here to the works of Jezebel in verse 22.

First, those who overcome will be given authority over the nations. In support of this a loose quote from Psalm 2:8-9, a messianic Psalm is given, probably chosen because the objects 'iron scepter' and 'pottery' had local significance in the life of Thyatirans.

This is another central motif in the Apocalypse. Those who overcome will actually have the privilege of ruling with the conquering Christ. He has been given authority over the nations and his rule is an everlasting one that will continue from age to age.

Everyone who overcomes and does the work of God is now given authority in a similar way as the Messiah himself. The authority he has received—the authority that belongs to him and him only—is now to be shared with those who remain faithful to the end. The faithful not only share in Christ's victory, but also in his never-ending rule. This is the first promise.

Second, those who overcome are given the morning star. This is another difficult symbol, much as the white stone in the previous letter. It may have had some local, even national significance in that the morning star was thought to represent Venus and was a symbol of sovereignty and victory. If it is used in this way it is further assurance that Christ, not Venus, is the victor and finally reigns over all, and this victory is also shared with and given to those who overcome (Rev. 22:16 shows Christ as morning star, or victor). This is the second promise.

What is given is important in this letter. First, we have Jezebel being given time to repent. Second, Christ gives to each according to their deeds. Third, in contrast to this, anyone who overcomes and does his works is given his authority and ultimate victory. "Let anyone who has an ear listen to what the Spirit says to the churches."

The Letter to Sardis (3:1-6)

Introduction

This ancient city was built on a steep hill and was known for its past wealth and commerce. In Sardis there were temples dedicated to Artemis and to Cybele, a goddess thought to have the power to bring the dead to life.

A secluded city, Sardis tended to lack vigilance as it was twice captured by enemies for failing to post guards at the city walls, an interesting parallel to the problem in the church. Seclusion often produces complacency, just as embracing the world produces compromise.

Many churches today are similar to this city. Attempts to seclude and separate proliferate, while there is a wholesale failure to post guards at hearts, minds and imaginations, which are deeply entrenched in worldly ways.

Text

(1-3) These words are spoken by the One who has the 'seven spirits of God.' This phrase, as understood back in 1:4, symbolizes the Holy Spirit (see also Zech. 4:1-10; Rev. 5:6). The seven stars are the angels of the seven churches (see 1:20).

The risen Christ knows the deeds of the church in Sardis. Their reputation is one of being alive, but in reality the community is dead. There may have been some evidence of life, but in verses 2-3 they are told with five imperatives that it is not sufficient. They were commanded to "Be watchful," "strengthen what remains," "remember what was received and heard," "keep it," and "repent." Their lives were characterized by a lack of completion, constantly falling short of full commitment and vigilance. They needed to turn from their complacency and re-orient their lives.

If the church at Sardis is not watchful they are warned that Christ will come to them in judgement. This probably should be thought of as present judgement, even though 'the thief coming' is a reference to final judgement in several contexts. Often in the Apocalypse this kind of language can refer to a visitation of judgement in the present, typologically prefiguring the final judgement. In any case, the second coming will come whether the church is watchful or not, and this seems to confirm the previous interpretation of a present judgment in this context.

(4) The word used here is 'yet' or 'nevertheless.' This time it is not an introduction to what Christ has against the church, but rather an

affirmation that there are some in the church who have not accommodated to the general laxness regarding pagan attitudes, lifestyles, and the church's half-hearted commitment to Christ. Those who have not adopted this way of life, but have held on to Christ wholeheartedly will walk with him dressed in white, a reference to those justified. Following the crucified and risen One is a task and joy that demands loyalty and faithfulness. "For they are worthy" refers to their justification through the work of Christ and to the fact that they have not done anything to jeopardize that position.

(5-6) There are three promises to those who overcome. First, they are promised to be dressed in white, or 'justified' before God (7:9, 10, 13-17). Second, the ones who overcome are never to be blotted out of the book of life; in other words, he/she has everlasting life. Third, is the promise that Christ will acknowledge their names before his Father and the angels. "Let anyone who has an ear listen to what the Spirit says to the churches."

Summary

The fourth and fifth letters to the churches in 2:18-3:6 have been analysed. Both letters, as in all the previous ones, affirm the speaker as Christ. In the letter to Thyatira he is described as the Son of God "whose eyes are like blazing fire and whose feet are like burnished bronze." He commends the church for her works, love, faith, and perseverance. However, there were some who were compromising with false teachings to the extent that Christ announces his imminent judgement if they do not repent. He instructs those who haven't compromised to hold on to what they have until he comes. The one who overcomes and does the works of Christ will be given a share of his authority over the nations.

The second letter is to Sardis. In this letter Christ is described as the holder of the seven spirits of God and the seven stars, both of which are referred to in chapter 1. Again, the presence of the risen Christ is emphasized in his words, "I know your deeds." Apparently the church at Sardis had a fine external reputation for being alive, but Christ says that in reality it is dead. They are admonished to, "Be watchful, strengthen what remains, remember what was received and heard, keep it and repent." They too are warned that if they are not watchful Christ will come to them in judgement. However, there are some in Sardis who have not fallen into complacency and away from commitment. They will walk with the risen Christ. Anyone who overcomes is promised everlasting life and acknowledgement by Christ before his Father.

The Letter to Philadelphia (3:7-13)

Introduction

Philadelphia was a smaller and more recently developed city than any of the other seven cities addressed in these letters. Because of its location it is often called the 'gateway to the East.' It was a fairly rich city with much productive agricultural land and some industry. Although destroyed by an earthquake, as was much of the region surrounding it in 17 CE, it was quickly rebuilt through imperial aid and its people remained loyal to the emperor. Temples dedicated to the imperial cult as well as many pagan gods were in prominence and Christians in this city were in a similar situation to the others John has already addressed.

Text

(7) The words of this letter are from "he who is holy and true." The risen Christ, as in the previous letters, addresses the church. Christ himself is called the Holy One. This was a common title used for God in the Old Testament and here it affirms Christ's deity. He is also the True One, an affirmation of his complete reliability. The One who is holy and true holds the key of David. What he opens no one can shut and what he shuts no one can open. This is a loose reference to Isaiah 22:22-25 and is likely to refer to the fact that Christ, who is holy and true, exercises authority over whoever enters the new Jerusalem, the proverbial dwelling place of God. We may also have a polemic against the Jews who were persecuting Christians in Philadelphia and seemingly attempting to exclude them from the household of God.

(8) As for the church at Philadelphia, we again have the statement that Christ is completely aware of its works. Similar to the letter to Smyrna, he doesn't have anything against believers here. The threat facing these churches in both letters is external, not internal. Both receive praise, not accusation.

The "open door" in verse 8, is likely to be a kind of parenthesis on the assessment of the church. It assures the Philadelphian Christians of Christ's absolute authority over entrance to heavenly Jerusalem in spite of their present rejection by the Jews. At the same time, it may also have been intended to encourage them to continue in missionary efforts, both in Philadelphia and other regions. Christ knows they are weak, but that in the midst of this they have not rejected his word, nor renounced his name, therefore he encourages them.

Let us think of ourselves in this context. In our own weakness we too must hold on to Christ's word and to his name. Even though we are weak (though usually not as a direct result of persecution), it is essential to realize that strength comes through holding on to Christ in these situations. The Philadelphians are an excellent example of Christians holding on, gritting it out, and standing firm in spite of having little strength.

(9) This reference to the Jews is similar to that which is in the letter to Smyrna. In both letters there is a conflict between those who are the people of God, namely the church, and those who claim to be the people of God, the Jews. Remember, in the New Testament a true Jew is a Christian. Those who claim to be Jews in this passage and are not are those who are not Christians. They are Jews in a physical sense, but not in a spiritual sense and will eventually acknowledge that Christians are the true people of God. Instead of all the nations coming to the feet of the Jews (Isa. 49:22-23), here we have a reversal of this prophecy in the sense that it is the nation of Israel—the physical descendents of Abraham—who now will come to realize that true Israel is the church, which Christ loves.

(10) Since they have held steadfast, the Philadelphian Christians are to be spared from the impending trial that is to come. "Those who live on the earth" is a phrase that is used many times in the Apocalypse to speak of those who are enemies of Christ and the church (6:10, 8:13, 11:10, 13:8). The coming hour of trial is to be a test of those who are not Christians. Yes, Christians will be persecuted and even martyred before Christ returns, but ultimately they are to be spared the wrath of God as he begins to destroy Satan. Christians are ultimately assured they will be spiritually protected through all that takes place.

(11) Another central motif that returns throughout the book is the promise: "I am coming soon." Christ will return with power and glory to complete his redeeming work and to consummate the rule of God, a rule which began in a unique way with his first coming. 'Soon' refers to a

prophetic view of salvation history. In the b part of verse 11 they are again instructed to hold on (a present imperative) to what they have. In this case, the instruction is probably a reference to keeping Christ's word, not denying his name and remaining steadfast. In other words, they are to hold fast to the integrity of their Christian lives so that no one will seduce or lure them away from victory.

(12-13) The one who overcomes will be given a secure place in the New Jerusalem. Philadelphia, remember, was located on ground that could not be trusted. Earthquakes forced people to abandon parts of the town and to live in outlying areas. The promise of a sure place in God's presence would have brought great assurance and it should continue to do for us in our present circumstances. Christ additionally promises to write the name of his God, his God's city, and his own new name on those who overcome. To have the name of God written on them shows that they 'belong' to God. The city, the New Jerusalem, written on them aims to show that they have citizenship in God's city. Having Christ's new name written on them infers seeing him in the fullness of who he is and this speaks of the special relationship of anyone who overcomes and the Christ who overcame. "Let anyone who has an ear listen to what the Spirit says to the churches."

The Letter to Laodicea (3:14-22)

Introduction

Laodicea was one of the wealthiest cities of its day. An example of the city's immense wealth was the city's refusal, after almost complete destruction by earthquake, of imperial aid to rebuild; they could afford to do it themselves. This city was known for its banks, its wool and textile industry which produced a special black wool, and for its medical school which developed an ear ointment and an eye salve.

Despite all its wealth, Laodicea was not completely self-sufficient. It seems that because of its location, the city was dependent on others for its water. The water was piped in through an aqueduct system that was fairly efficient for its day, but the quality of some of the water was less than desirable. As we study the letter it is important to keep these details in mind.

Text

(**14**) In the salutation of this letter we have the usual identification of the speaker. The speaker's description is not as clearly connected to chapter 1, as it is in all the previous letters, but there is an allusion to 1:2 that is not to be missed.

The words here are, "Amen, the faithful and true witness, the ruler of God's creation." The application of the word 'Amen' to Christ signifies that he, as God in the Old Testament, is trustworthy and completely reliable. 'Faithful and true witness' seems to re-enforce this contrast between Christ and the Laodecian church. The last phrase, "the ruler or beginning of God's creation" has a close connection with Colossians 1:15-18. We have clear evidence that the Laodicean church, located about ten miles from Colossae, had read the letter addressed to the Colossians (Col. 4:16). The concern in both Paul's hymn and the phrase here is to emphasize Christ's lordship over all. Christ is the Amen, the faithful and true witness, and Lord over all creation.

(**15**) As in all the other letters it is made clear that the risen Christ knows the deeds of the church in Laodicea. In this case, there is no particular fault-finding in relationship to pagan activity as in some of the previous letters. Rather, the grievance is that the Laodiceans are neither hot nor cold; the desire is that they be one or the other.

This terminology brings us back to the water supply, or lack thereof, at Laodicea. In the introduction we noted that Laodicea was dependent on others for its water. There were two prominent sources or types of water in close proximity—that of Hierapolis, which was hot and medicinal, and that of Colossae which was cold and pure.

(16) The Laodicean church, because it is lukewarm is about to literally be vomited (a violent metaphor) out of Christ's mouth. It is important to realize that both *hot* and *cold* are a contrast to *lukewarm*, but not to each other! *Hot* and *cold* then are not positive and negative descriptions, but both are positive in regard to what the church's works should be. It is often thought that hot means 'going all out for the Lord' or a full commitment, while cold means, 'no passion for the Lord' or no commitment. If this is the case, the question we're faced with is why Christ would approve of no commitment at all?

The fact of the matter is the church's works are neither hot in a healing sense, nor cold in a spiritual sense. The church is clearly unproductive, and therefore Christ is about to vomit them out of his mouth. They are being called to accountability for their lack of works and it is in this sense that Christ wishes they were hot or cold, either one will do, but sadly they are lukewarm and therefore distasteful to him.

(17-18) The distinction between hot or cold, and lukewarm shares a contrast with presuming to be rich and truly being rich. Verse 17 shows something of the Laodicean lukewarmness and this may have accounted for their lack of Christian work. They have lost the ability to be self critical and therefore have a distorted view of themselves in relation to Christ.

The solution to this problem is to buy, metaphorically, from Christ true riches: gold that has been refined and made pure, white clothes of righteousness to cover their nakedness, and eye salve so they might see. This solution refers to the local banking center, wool industry, and medical school aiming to touch the Laodiceans where they live and to give them a new view of themselves.

(19) A principle occurring many times in scripture is that rebuking, confrontation, and discipline are expressions of Christ's love. In light of this, Christians are to repent—a one time act—that turns them back in the right direction, and to continually be passionate in following in the footsteps of the crucified and risen One.

(20) The flip side of the love mentioned in verse 19 is demonstrated by this same Christ who is willing to stand at the gate and knock, awaiting a response from the one who hears his voice. Christ standing at the gate is not a threat, but a promise.

No doubt this imagery would have jolted the church. Its city entrances and exits were sealed by gates denying entrance to potential adversaries. Christ stands at the gate knocking, awaiting a welcome response. If anyone hears his voice and opens the gate he assures them that his or her hospitality will not be abused or taken advantage of, as might be the case with corrupt Roman officials.

The crucified and risen One still passionately cares for the Laodicean church in spite of its lukewarm state. He loves it enough to confront it, call for its repentance, and to promise anyone who invites him in a renewed experience of intimate community.

Perhaps, in the b part of this verse there is an allusion to the future messianic banquet where those from all tribes and nations will sit with the Messiah and share a meal. If so, this is in the present, a foretaste of the future where the future breaks into the present through the intimacy of sharing a meal together with Christ. This reality of active community should grow greater and greater in its intensity as we realize 'the presence of the future' in each of our lives and in the world in which we live.

(21-22) The future is promised to anyone who overcomes. As Christ overcame and sat with his Father on his throne, so all who overcome will share in this victory and rule. "Let anyone who has an ear listen to what the Spirit says to the churches."

THE HEAVENLY COURT, THE LAMB, & THE SCROLL (1) (4:1-5:14)

Introduction

In chapter 4 John introduces us to a magnificent *throne theophany*. There were a number of these in the Old Testament. A throne theophany is a vision of God seated on a throne surrounded by his heavenly host or court.

This type of vision frequently occurs in a prophet's call and it is probably fair to assume this is one of its functions for the writer, John, who stands in the stream of prophets God has raised up throughout the generations.

Another function of the chapter is to direct attention to God, and to portray him as the Holy King, Creator of the universe, and the One who is worthy of worship. This God is the One who was, is, and is to come. Almighty God, the potentate of time, is ruling and the Apocalypse aims to target this truth and develop it so that believers would live in faith and trust.

In the battle of sovereignties that continues to be present today, he is currently and will continue to be in the future the everlasting victor.

However fearful or overwhelming the forces of evil become, God has assured the victory for himself and his people.

One of the most difficult issues we all face is trusting God. When times are good or bad, trust can wane. These explosive visions are a potent reminder that God is trustworthy, and he merits our trust and allegiance in every situation.

Text

i) 4:1-11

(1) This chapter begins with a formulaic "After this I looked," or better "saw," a phrase used many times in the Apocalypse to announce a new or separate part of a vision (7:1, 15:5, 18:1). John sees before him an open door in heaven (the term 'heaven' can mean different things depending on the context). The open door suggests that either John could see through it or that he actually goes through it to be shown all that is taking place. The connotation of the phrase implies that John is privileged to a direct revelation of the highest standard.

As in 1:10, John hears the voice like a trumpet speaking to him. This is symbolic language and the speaker is the risen Christ. Again, we can see how we must not force John to conform to our standard of literalness. For him there is fluidity with concreteness.

The quote from the risen Christ in the c part of the verse, "Come up here, and I will show you what must take place after this," is often used to support the idea of a rapture of the church at this time. In this view John represents all Christians, and the trumpet is the voice heard at Parousia. Contextually, one is hard-pressed to see either John's intent or the textual evidence affirming such a view. This type of interpretation imposes a grid on the text and only gets out of it that which has gone into it.

In addition to this passage being interpreted as a reference to the rapture, some understand this quote to be a reference to what is solely future. As I pointed out in 1:19, this neat division of the vision in 1:9-20 representing past events, the seven letters in 2:1-3:22 representing present events, and 4:1-22:21 representing future events is helpful to a point, but shouldn't be thought of as absolute and fixed. For example, the letters are not concerned solely with the present to the exclusion of the future or the past. It seems to me the same type of interweaving of past, present, and future continues throughout the Apocalypse. To refer to these chapters (4:1-22:21) as futuristic is not entirely wrong, but to refer to them as exclusively futuristic makes too much out of this verse and goes against the rest of the evidence in the text itself.

(2-3) Similar to 1:10, John describes himself here as "in the Spirit" (Ezk. 11:1, 5). In doing so, he links his vision with those of the prophets of the Old Testament. This revelation is not of his own intuition or creation, but comes to him in a state that transcends the norm for all Christians. John is writing prophecy in the tradition of those who had previously revealed God's word.

While he is 'in the Spirit' John sees the throne in heaven with someone sitting on it (Isa. 6; Ezk. 1:28, 3:1-3). In verses 3 ff he gives a description of what he sees. In the Apocalypse the word 'throne' occurs forty-seven times out of sixty-two in the entire New Testament, no doubt indicating a polemic against the thrones of the emperor and pagan deities. John is seeing, and showing, that there is a throne in heaven above all others, an everlasting throne from which Almighty God rules over history ultimate closure.

In terms of a description of God, John speaks less of the form of God than Ezekiel, and records his impressions in terms of colors of precious stones. It is probably fair to think of jasper and carnelian emphasizing the majesty and brilliance of God enthroned, while the rainbow may be a reminder of his covenant with humanity in Genesis 9.

(4) From this point on we should begin to feel more hard-pressed as to the precise meaning of the author's symbolism. The twenty-four thrones and elders have been the subject of much discussion. Some argue that the twenty-four elders are an angelic order which comprise what is often part of Old Testament throne theophanies—the heavenly court or host (Ps. 89:7; 1 Kings 22:19). The number twenty-four relates to the twenty-four priestly and Levitical orders functioning here as the heavenly host.

Others hold, with slightly different nuances, that the twenty-four elders are not angels, but the twelve patriarchs of the nation of Israel and the twelve apostles of the New Testament. Limited support for this may be found in Rev. 21:12 ff where the names of the twelve tribes of Israel are written on the gates of the New Jerusalem and the names of the twelve apostles on the twelve foundations of the city.

(5) As the scene turns us back to the throne, several symbols are associated with the power and majesty of God. Seven lamps of fire, which are identified as the seven spirits of God (also 1:4, 3:1, and in 5:6) appear before the throne. The latter phrase only occurs these four times in all of Scripture and never in Jewish writings, making it especially difficult to decode the symbolism. As was suggested in 1:4, perhaps the background is Zechariah 4:1-10, and the author has incorporated the meaning of this imagery from there. It seems possible then that the seven spirits symbolically designate the Holy Spirit and intend to give a broader range to the Spirit's function and work.

In relation to this, chapter 4 proclaims the Father's everlasting nature, holiness, and power, while chapter 5 proclaims the Lamb as King and Savior. It would be fitting if the seven spirits in the original context (chapters 4-5) were the Holy Spirit.

(6-10) John describes 'what looked like' a clear sea of glass. He again speaks symbolically and without precision. The Old Testament imagery (Ex. 24:10; Ezk.1:22, 26) seems to reinforce the awesome holiness of God and the distance between Creator and creature this holiness necessitates.

The imagery of the four living creatures around the throne is undoubtedly reminiscent of Ezekiel 1 and Isaiah 6, but modified by John. The creatures here have one face, whereas in Ezekiel they have four each. In both cases though, the likenesses are the same. They are described as a lion, ox, man, and eagle. In this context it seems most appropriate to see these creatures as heavenly beings, perhaps of an angelic order. In any case, the verse indicates they are close to God and his throne, praising and worshipping him night and day.

A description of the creatures continues. They are covered with eyes, suggesting their awareness of all that is taking place. In the latter part of the verse the continuous worship and praise implied in "day and night" probably shouldn't be taken too literally. Verse 9 puts it in perspective by equating 'when or whenever' with 'at any time.' The proclamation by the four creatures comes from Isaiah 6:3, with the last line modified to suit the Apocalypse in giving assurance of God's past, present, and future identity.

Those facing severe persecution in the churches would surely have taken great comfort in the fact that God is holy and almighty. He is, was, and is to come. The holy, almighty God has begun to and will finally triumph over all evil. Each time the living creatures give glory, honor, and thanks to God, the twenty-four elders bow down and worship. God is described as the one who lives forever and ever and who is on the throne. The repetition serves to assure those facing terrible persecution and to remind them that God is reigning over the emperor and pagan gods. The act of the elders placing their crowns before the throne probably intends to affirm this.

(11) Verse 11 closes the chapter with the elders proclaiming to God, "He is worthy and he is the Lord God." These two liturgical praises were frequently used in reference to the emperor. Here, the elders proclaim that God is worthy to receive glory, honor, and power as it is he who created all things by his will. Whether we face violent or a subtle persecution, we too must be willing to trust God and to continue to proclaim him and him alone as worthy. He is Creator of the universe and is worthy to be on the throne. God is not some disinterested party; he has not forsaken the world or his people. He is bringing history to its ultimate consummation: the defeat of Satan and evil, the final judgement, and the new heavens and earth.

THE HEAVENLY COURT, THE LAMB & THE SCROLL (2) 4:1-5:14

Introduction

In the previous chapter we explored chapter 4 and were given a glimpse of a vision of God enthroned, a very similar picture to Old Testament throne theophanies usually found in the context of a prophet's call. John seems to be saying in recording these visions that he too stands in the stream of those who receive prophetic revelation.

The vision John is privileged to see is one of God's majesty. We saw the Old Testament influence on John from Ezekiel and Isaiah, and the similar yet modified descriptions.

God is proclaimed as three times holy; he is the Almighty who was, who is, and who is to come. God is everlasting in his power, majesty, and holiness as opposed to the frailty and finiteness of human emperors or pagan gods. This God is worthy of praise for he has created all things. His throne is above all and there are none that can be compared to him.

This magnificent throne theophany proceeds with the seven-sealed scroll coming into this awesome picture. The heightening drama of no one being able to open the scroll aims to direct readers to the Lamb and his sacrificial work of salvation.

In all heaven and earth, only he is found worthy to open the scroll with its seven seals. Drama cuts to the core of who we are and these remarkable scenes are intended to do no less than open us up to the reality of the living God in his majesty and salvific action on behalf of his people.

Text

ii) 5:1-14

(1) Chapter 5 is a continuation of the vision in chapter 4, where John still sees God enthroned and holding a sealed scroll with seven seals in his right hand. The imagery is reminiscent of Ezekiel 2:9-10 which also refers to a scroll with writing on both sides.

(2-4) A mighty angel poses the question: "Who is worthy to break the seals and open the scroll?" According to verse 3 no one in the whole universe is worthy to look inside the scroll. The search seems to have failed and John weeps at the prospect of the contents of the scroll remaining sealed.

(5-6) One of the elders of chapter 4 says to John, "Do not weep." Why does the elder sense a need for reassurance? The scroll will indeed be opened as there is one who has proved to be worthy. He is described as "the Lion of the tribe of Judah and the Root of David." These two phrases should be understood as messianic. There is an interweaving of the two, showing that it is the Messiah who is victorious.

However, the Messiah was neither the political ruler of Jewish expectation nor the forerunner of God's *immediate* end time judgement as John the Baptist thought. He was rather the suffering servant, which verses 6 ff make clear. He is the fulfiller of the Old Testament in both who he is and what he has accomplished.

Three things should be mentioned about the Lamb. First, the Lamb is *slain*. The *sacrificial* language here graphically describes the Lamb as having its throat cut. Second, the Lamb is standing, alluding to the resurrection and pointing out that death was not the end of this Lamb's mission. The Lamb is standing near the throne, encircled by the creatures and the elders, signifying the centrality of the Lamb's status. Before we move on to the third description, we begin to understand something of the radical imagery in verses 5 and 6. A *slain messiah* was something not even John the Baptist was expecting. We have then not a warrior Lion, but a conquering Lamb, a Passover Lamb, and a risen Redeemer, who is deemed worthy to open the scroll.

The third observation is that the Lamb has seven horns and seven eyes which are the seven spirits of God sent out into the earth. Horns are a frequent symbol of power in the Old Testament, but also are used to enforce the idea of authority and royalty. The number seven, as elsewhere in the Apocalypse, most likely denotes completeness and perfection. The seven eyes and therefore the seven spirits of God (5:6) remind us of similar imagery in Zech. 4:1-10. In both cases the spirits are sent into the earth and most likely refer to the Holy Spirit.

(7-8) The Lamb, the only one authorized to do so, comes to take the scroll from God and open it. Once the scroll is in the Lamb's possession, the creatures and elders fall down to praise him. If it is appropriate to refer to this part of the vision as an enthronement ceremony, now is when it reaches its culmination with the Lamb enthroned and receiving praise.

The elders' harps are notably instruments of worship and adoration, appearing again in 14:2 and 15:2, for the Lamb taking the scroll from God is a great occasion. It is a celebration of awe and wonder in which the heavenly host can do nothing but fall and worship.

Both the characterization of the golden bowls full of incense and the prayers of the saints have an Old and New Testament affiliation. In Psalm 141:2 and Luke 1:10 there is a connection between incense and prayer, affirming the traditional ritual significance of this picture. Here the elders do not play a mediatorial role, but rather one of presentation.

(9-12) Those in heaven sing a new song to the Lamb who is worthy because of the accomplished sacrifice, the blood which has ransomed people for God from every tribe, nation, language, and people. The Lamb has redeemed sinners and is victorious over sin and death. Those who are redeemed are a kingdom of priests able to serve God. It is important not to see a 'kingdom' as identical to 'the kingdom of God' or 'the kingdom of Heaven' as recorded in the synoptic gospels. There is undoubtedly some overlap, but the two are not the same thing. A 'kingdom' is a group of people while 'the Kingdom of God/Heaven' is most frequently a phrase referring to the rule of God.

The redeemed then have been purchased for God to serve him and to reign with him. As God's rule has broken into the present through the mission and ministry of the Lamb and begun moving towards consummation, the redeemed are assured of final victory and a share in God's everlasting rule. The living creatures and the elders are now joined by a countless number of angels who sing or chant the doxology praising the Lamb. "Worthy is the Lamb who was slain" repeats what has been sung in verse 9 while the next four attributes (power, wealth, wisdom, and strength) emphasize this worthiness.

(13-14) The ceremony is brought to a close with the whole created order recognizing the authority of God and the Lamb. This is neither universalism nor personal redemption, but rather an assurance that nothing in the universe stands outside the ultimate triumph of the Lamb to the glory of God.

The four living creatures pronounce the 'Amen.' This fitting liturgical expression puts the stamp of approval on the truth claims that have been revealed in chapters 4 and 5. These two chapters have put things in place for us. In chapter 4 John is privileged to receive the Apocalypse 'in the Spirit' in startling visionary form. He sees God as enthroned, a throne theophany with all its Old Testament significance and wonder. At the same time the chapter functions as a type of 'call narrative' having many of the same characteristics of prophetic calls in the Old Testament and emphasizing John's standing within the stream of receiving prophetic visions and revelation.

The vision of God enthroned is a vision of the God who is holy, almighty, and who was, is, and is to come. He lives forever and ever. He is worthy for he has created all things. In this scene there is assurance that those facing dire circumstances and life-threatening persecution can trust God. He is holy, almighty, and everlasting. In a world that may seem to be out of control, in a world of suffering and death he is there, moving history forward to its sure and final cataclysmic consummation.

In chapter 5 John's vision continues. The high drama in the first 4 verses is resolved in verses 5 ff. The scroll with its seven seals will not remain unopened. The Lamb with its throat cut—in fact *because* of its throat being cut—is deemed worthy to open the scroll. He is to be praised.

Again, the scene depicts great and glorious assurance. In a world where we often become pessimistic, hopeless, and powerless, those of us who have been cleansed from sin by the blood of the Lamb must remember his blood has purchased us for God; we are his. This is no other-worldly theory, but a profound historical-theological truth we must embrace and live out. We too are not to weep, but to take courage, to be comforted and assured. The Lamb has triumphed and his victory is ours to share.

OPENING THE SIX SEALS (6:1-17)

Introduction

Chapters 4 and 5 set the scene for what follows. Chapter 4 emphasized that God is enthroned and supreme over all. He is proclaimed as holy and almighty, worthy as creator of the universe.

In the same vision in chapter 5, the seven-sealed scroll is in the right hand of him who sits on the throne. The heightening drama here is instantly recognizable. No one in all heaven or earth was found worthy to open or even look in the scroll. John, while weeping, is told there is One after all who has triumphed.

The Lion of the tribe of Judah, the Root of David, is able to open the scroll and unseal the seals. John sees the Lamb (*slain* but *standing*), who comes and takes the scroll from the One on the throne.

Once this is accomplished there is an outburst of praise affirming the worthiness of the Lamb. The Lamb was slain, thereby making the necessary sacrifice for sin, purchasing people for God as only this Lamb could. Chapter 5 concludes with praise and adoration to God and to the Lamb.

It is crucial to have the revelatory visions of both chapters 4 and 5 in our minds as we explore chapter 6 in more detail. God is enthroned and the Lamb is in his glorious presence. With the drama now resolved in 5:6-8 and the slain, but standing Lamb opening the scroll, the outcome of the first six of the seven seals now becomes available.

Text

i) 6:1-17

(1) John is watching as the Lamb opens the first seal. One of the four creatures announces the imperative, "Come." Many understand this command to be addressed to John; it is better to see it as a summons to the horsemen as is shown by their instant appearance in verses 2, 4, 5, 8 (see also Zech. 6:1-3).

(2) Next John sees a white horse and a rider holding a bow. The rider is given a crown and rides out to conquer. There is a dispute as to the identity of this rider. Many see the rider here as Christ. However, this seems unlikely, as it is the Lamb who is opening the seals. For him to appear as one of the four horsemen doesn't quite fit the context or the setting of the vision. Others argue that this first rider represents the forward-moving power of the gospel. This also seems unlikely, as there is no indication of that in the context. It is more likely that the rider represents war or a conqueror bent on conquest. The immediate contextual hint of this is the bow. Old Testament prophets use numerous allusions to bows, symbolic for military power (Hos. 1:5; Hab. 3:8-9; Ezk. 5:1-17).

(3-4) As the second seal is opened with the repeated imperative 'Come,' we are told this time the horse is red. The rider is given power to take peace from the earth and cause people to slay each other. The second seal takes the first seal further in that the effects of war are deepened and there is no peace on earth. It is possible that we have in these first two seals both invasions from external enemies as well as internal strife: a civil war resulting in the slaughtering of one's own people.

(5-6) The third seal is opened and the imperative calls for the black horse and a rider holding a scale. This is likely to represent a shortage of food. Notice how carefully the food is measured and distributed. The price demanded for a quart of wheat is astronomical, perhaps twelve times the norm. The barley, less nutritious and cheaper than wheat, will only bring three quarts for a day's wages. The point is that food is available for people. It seems there is a situation of shortage; famine or starvation is not an issue. This is supported by the next words, "do not damage the oil and wine." Neither is a part of the shortage this time. What we have here are partial shortages that begin to announce an ever worsening, but not yet catastrophic situation.

(7-11) The fourth seal is opened. The fourth horse, pale like a corpse and its rider are called forth. The rider's name is Death, and Hades is close behind. They are given power over a fourth of the earth to kill through sword, famine, plagues, and wild beasts. This is showing again a partial picture of a potentially more disastrous situation.

The last rider of the four deepens the perspective of the first three, as the opening of the fourth seal combines and extends the meaning of the previous three seals. Death is ushered in with his accomplice lurking in the background.

The fifth seal has now been opened. This time there is no imperative. Instead of a horse and rider, John sees the souls of the martyrs under the altar. This brings us back to one of the central motifs in the Apocalypse, the suffering and persecution of God's people. The martyrs are 'under the altar.' This phrase is perhaps best understood in close association with Old Testament sacrifice. The blood of an animal was thought to be its life or soul and was poured out at the base of the altar (Lev. 4:7, 17:11). This could be a way of saying those slain 'under the altar' are those who have been unwilling to denounce God. They have become sacrifices on the altar because of their testimony and witness to his word.

The martyrs cry out to God, "How long before your judgement? How long before our blood is avenged?" This is a cry for ultimate justice, not limited personal revenge, and is based on the fact that God is holy and true and that the martyrs have been slain for his word. Their call is that God would reverse the illegitimate judgement put upon his people by 'the inhabitants of the earth' (which, as we've seen, is a phrase depicting those on earth who are God's enemies and persecutors of his people).

In response to their cry they are each given a white robe. This is a sign of their justification in God's eyes as opposed to the illegitimate judgement imposed upon them which resulted in their deaths. They are told to be patient a while longer for the persecution of God's people is not yet finished and there will be others who will be cut down for their faith. In the ongoing battle of sovereignties, the rule of God continues to move towards consummation. As the battle continues there will be casualties, but those in Christ will be given white robes of justification and ultimate victory over their oppressors.

We must remind ourselves again of the historical context. Many Christians were suffering persecution and imminent death. The cry, 'How long?' resonates as a part of their experience on earth, much as it does with us today. We too must listen to the reply, "be patient a little longer." In our consumer driven age the Western church is patient for nothing. Mimicking our culture, we have lost the notion that patiently waiting is an essential virtue for followers of the crucified and risen One.

(12-14) The sixth seal is now opened. In apocalyptic terms we are given a description of what the martyrs have requested in verse 10. In symbolic language, the cosmic catastrophes (Joel 2:10) all point to God's impending judgement. Various signs—earthquakes, the blackened sun, the blood-red moon, stars falling to earth (Isa. 34:14), the sky rolling up as a scroll, mountains and islands removed from their places—all speak of a divine visitation in judgement (Jer. 4:24). Order in the cosmos seems to be shattering as the universe itself spins into chaos. The next verses show that John sees these previous verses as more symbolic than literal, because both his Revelation and life continue before the divine visitation in judgement makes God's enemies seek escape from so great a terror (Isa. 2:11).

(15-17) John first mentions seven groups of people from the greatest to the weakest. They all seek escape among the mountains, even to the point of calling out to the rocks to fall on them and hide them (Hos. 10:8), perhaps even kill them so as to avoid the wrath of God and the Lamb. 'The great day' of wrath has come, and begun judging who is able to stand.

In the midst of their own difficult circumstances John assures his readers that those who are against God and the Lamb, those persecuting their own people, will not stand. There is only one Emperor. God is mightier than all counterfeits, whether they take the form of pagan gods or human kings.

TWO MULTITUDES (7:1-17)

Introduction

Often referred to as a prelude, interlude, or parenthesis, chapter 7 is sandwiched between the opening of the sixth and seventh seals. It does, in some sense, seem to answer the question posed in 6:17: "In the great day of wrath who can stand?" Overall, this chapter is one of assurance in the midst of terror. However, we are left with several questions concerning some of the details. For example, are the two parts of the chapter, verses 1-8 and 9-17, connected to one another or should they be thought of as separate? Who are the 144,000 and what are we to make of the description of them being sealed? Of course, concerning these questions and others in this chapter there are wide varieties of opinions and suggestions. Let us then get into the text and see if we can better understand it together.

Text

i) 7:1-8

(1) John sees four angels stationed at the four corners of the earth, conveying the idea that the corners of the whole world depict earthly limits that nothing extends beyond. They are seen as holding back the "four winds of the earth" a phrase often used in the Old Testament to symbolize destruction (Jer. 49:36 ff; Zech. 6:5). We can hypothesize that John may have seen a motif-related connection between the four winds and the four horsemen of the previous chapter. Both represent coming destruction; therefore, perhaps we should not think of these four winds as some new or different destruction, but as essentially that which takes place in 6:1-8. In addition, if this understanding of the four winds is connected sequentially, we should place this vision prior to the six seals. John's visions are not always recorded in chronological order; structural emphasis is placed on the fluidity in his style and message.

(2-8) The prophet sees another angel (a Christlike figure) who addresses the other four. This angel enters the scene from the east; most likely representing the thought that God's glory comes from the east (Ezk. 43:2-4). This angel has the *seal* of the 'living God.' The fact that God is a living God is often mentioned in the Old Testament, contrasting the one true God with the surrounding pagan gods. The intention here is similar.

Now let us look a little more carefully at the seal. The language John uses in these verses also recalls Ezekiel 9. This Old Testament passage depicts the impending judgement about to come upon Jerusalem for its idolatry. Looking ahead to 9:4, the man clothed in linen is told to put a seal on those who lament Jerusalem's sin. In 9:5-6 we see the effect of having this seal, which in this context probably resembled something close to a cross. Those who have it are not touched by the terror and destruction of God's wrath coming in judgement.

The function of a seal was well-known in these times. Rulers in the ancient East often used a seal to put their stamp on certain writings or treaties to protect them against destruction. These functions of the seal and stamp are connected to our text. The aim of a seal is to protect, secure, and to signify one's stamp of ownership. The Holy Spirit fills this role of impression on believers who belong to God. The aim of the seal is to mark God servants, preserving them from his impending wrath.

The next question is "Who are these servants?" *Servants* is a plural here, with no clear indication of a particular group that is to receive the seal. Tentatively, we can suggest that all God's servants are meant. However, words are used in contexts and the context here (as we go on to see in verse 4) speaks of 144,000 as the number sealed from all the tribes of Israel. Does the number of those sealed have anything to do with the identity of these servants? To answer this question we need to look at this paragraph (verses 4-8) in more detail.

First of all, the tribes are listed in a slightly unusual way:

(1) The tribe of Judah is named first; this is unusual because traditionally Reuben, as Jacob's firstborn, is mentioned first. This change is striking. It seems quite likely that Judah is listed first because this is the tribe from which the Messiah came.
(2) Another striking change in this list is the omitting of Dan, who is otherwise usually listed. Following the lead of other biblical commentators, I would suggest that a plausible explanation is that Dan is omitted because of this tribe's tendency to engage itself in idolatry. In some way all the tribes, more or less, could be excluded on these grounds, but the tribe of Dan was

particularly notorious for idol worship. In addition, early tradition argued that the antichrist would descend from the tribe of Dan (rabbinic interpretation of Gen. 49:17; Jer. 8:16).

(3) In relation to this, notice that Manasseh is part of the group. This is again unusual because Manasseh is part of the tribe of Joseph. The explanation of this may lie in the desire of the scribe to complete the list, bringing the number again to twelve after the omission of Dan.

The second thing we need to explore is the number twelve. There are twelve tribes and the 12,000 sealed from each tribe. Why 12,000, and why twelve tribes rather than ten or eleven? It would seem the number twelve is used in this context in a symbolic sense, much like the sacred number seven, and stands for completeness. Examples of this number are frequent in the Apocalypse as in the twelve tribes: 12,000 sealed from each tribe; the New Jerusalem whose sides measure 12,000 furlongs and which has twelve gates with the names of the twelve tribes (21:12 ff), guarded by the twelve angels, with twelve foundations with the name of the twelve apostles. I could continue, but I think you get the point.

Finally, we must consider those who are sealed. We need to decide how John is applying these verses and to whom. There are several possibilities:

Some interpret this passage to mean that those sealed are literally Jews, physical Israel. If this is the case, there would be a contrast here with the great multitude in verse 9 making the problem with this view its selectivity. The difficulty with seeing those who are sealed as a reference to literal Jews comes in verse 3, which mentions those to be sealed as "servants of God," strongly implying that they are Christians. In John's eyes Jews would have no longer, outside of Christ, been understood to be serving God (contrast Rev. 2:9, 3:8-9).

Another possibility here is that these are Jewish Christians. This position doesn't quite fit because it's too selective, implying that only these Jewish Christians are sealed against the coming destruction. As a result, Gentile Christians, while being 'servants of God,' would not receive the seal.

A third possibility is that the 144,000 are the portion of the whole church that is to be martyred. I find this possibility more plausible than the first two, but am still not convinced. The selectivity goes against the imagery of the sealing which is for protection from God's wrath, not martyrdom.

The fourth and last possibility seems the most likely. It's possible that John intends to say that it is the whole church which is sealed, not a select group at the time of the coming destruction. This connects with what we've previously seen in the Apocalypse—a true Jew is a Christian.

This perspective also squares with the wider context of the whole New Testament as Paul refers to the church as the true Israel in Romans 2:29, and James speaks to the church as the twelve tribes in James 1:1. Perhaps, it is appropriate to say that John is using a past association to point typologically to a present reality. True Israel is the church; they are the spiritual Israel, for the true church follows the Messiah.

Therefore, each member of each tribe is sealed or marked in protection from God's wrath. All of God's servants will receive the seal. This inclusiveness is emphasized by the naming of the twelve tribes and the repeating of the number 12,000 after each tribe, showing in the strongest possible way that this is a complete sealing. None of those who are God's will be left unprotected from danger. God shelters and protects his people!

ii) 7:9-17

(9) What takes place in verse 9 is the eventual result of the inclusive sealing. The great multitude is from every tribe, nation, language, and

people. This great multitude may refer to all believers throughout time and not just the sealed, but as the vision goes on to point out, the special emphasis is on those who are the complete church being sealed at this time. Ultimately, all God's people will be protected from his wrath and eventually stand before the throne and in front of the Lamb as they are. They will do so wearing white robes with palm branches in their hands, a sign of being justified and victorious with the Lamb.

(10-12) The multitude cries out, "Salvation belongs to God and to the Lamb!" In other words, thousands of angels, the elders and the living creatures, as well as the whole host of heaven now burst forth in praise to God. The first 'Amen' probably affirms the first liturgical pronouncement, while the second confirms the seven-fold doxology directed to God.

(13-14) John is now addressed concerning "these in white robes." Who are they? Where did they come from? He politely puts the elder on the spot, suggesting the answer to the question is known to the asker. At the same time, John shows his own uncertainty and dependence on being shown what is being revealed.

'These in white robes' are said to have come out of the great tribulation. The emphasis is perhaps not so much on *exclusivity* as on *especially* in this reference. The elder is speaking *primarily* of those who go through the intensification of tribulation just before the end of the end in the following chapters. However, we probably should not narrow the scope too far here as if there is no tribulation until the end of the end is upon us. In some sense tribulation is represented by messianic woes, suffering, and persecution which have been with the church since Christ's death and will remain with her until his return. There will indeed be a deepening of such trials, perhaps even in some cases to the point of death, but both victory and justification are the assured result of the sacrificial cleansing and redemptive work achieved by the Lamb.

(15-17) We find here the great salvific promise of standing before the throne of God, enjoying direct access and community. God will be his people's very shelter and comfort. The section closes with the fulfilment of promises spoken to Israel on its restoration from exile in Isaiah 49:10. Whatever torment God's people face, they will be free from it; whatever their need or desire, they will be completely satisfied. This glorious reality of wholeness and completeness, protection and safety, exists because the Lamb is at the center of the throne and he will be their shepherd leading them to springs of living water. God will wipe every tear from the eyes of his people. There will be no suffering, no weeping over death, no catastrophes or disasters. God's rule is consummated. The Lamb is at the center of the throne and the church is in the very presence of God and the Lamb.

The words of these visions no doubt brought great assurance to God's people in John's own day. We must not lose sight of the fact that the Apocalypse is addressed to the seven churches in Asia. It was relevant to their own situation as well as it is to ours in the present and future. They found themselves surrounded by pagan gods, emperor worship, and a general hostility towards Christians. Much of the same is with us today. What is our response?

These visions revealed to John, and then to God's people in written form, aim to show the ultimate destiny of the people of God, regardless of the immediate circumstances. They are to share in community with the Lamb and God, to be redeemed and saved forever, rather than to face God's inevitable wrath. Here we have a beautiful picture of the reality of God's intimate and personal care for his people. Don't let this picture and its reality leave you untouched. We who are God's must embrace this truth and live on the basis of his wonderful grace and mercy, remembering the fact that we can and will one day wash our robes, making them white in the blood of the Lamb.

THE SEVENTH SEAL & THE SIX TRUMPETS (1) (8:1-9:21)

General Review

Before beginning chapter 8 let us quickly review chapters 4, 5, 6, and 7. In chapter 4 John sees God enthroned in majesty. Verse 8 declares him the Holy, Lord God Almighty, who was, who is, and who is to come. In 5:7 the slain Lamb comes to take the scroll from God. In verse 9, the Lamb, for he was slain and with his blood purchased people for God, is declared worthy to take the scroll and to open it. The end of the verse shows us the extent of the purchase. People from every tribe, language, and nation are included in the redemptive work of the Lamb. Chapter 5 ends with great praise and worship being given to the One who sits on the throne and to the Lamb.

Chapter 6 portrays the Lamb opening the sealed scroll. The first four seals correspond to the four horsemen and the coming destruction they are about to inflict on the earth. The fifth seal is related to the martyrs, those slain because of their witness to the word of God. Their cry goes out, "How long, Sovereign Lord, holy and true, before your judgement?"

The sixth seal affirms the impending judgement in graphic language aiming to show what God coming in judgement will be like. This directly relates to verses 15 ff showing the extent of this judgement. The wrath of God and the Lamb are imminent. In that great day who can stand?

Chapter 7 gives us the response to that question. All God's servants will be able to stand in the face of his coming wrath. They are assured their protection on the earth will result in their standing before the throne and in the front of the Lamb in a new heavens and earth. Reading the promises of being in God's presence in verses 16-17 is a tremendous comfort.

Introduction

After the interlude of chapter 7, we now move into chapters 8-9 in which the seventh seal is opened and the six trumpets sounded. Remember that chapters 8 and 9 contain a high degree of literary artistry. John does not intend to give us a chronological narrative. There is progression, but not chronology. This series of visions repeats and deepens that which has already been thematically introduced. Manifestations of the wrath of God and the Lamb are coming upon the world. The wickedness of human beings does not pass by God without his notice and God can, has, and will work against sin and its devastating effects.

Text

i) 8:1-5

(**1-2**) The seventh seal is opened and upon its opening, there is silence in heaven. How are we to understand this silence? There are several suggestions. It could simply be a 'dramatic pause' as all heaven stands in awe of the imminent judgement of God. Or possibly the silence is a return to 'absolute stillness,' which existed at creation. This second view finds support in many Jewish apocalypses in relation to their expectation of God's judgement (2 Esdras 7:29 ff). However, there is yet a third option, which fits the context better. There is silence in heaven because of the significance of the prayers of the saints. The angels, in verse 2, are given trumpets, but they do not prepare to blow them until verse 6. Placing the action here rather than at the end of verse 2 emphasizes the fact that the sounding of the trumpets is awaiting God's reception of the prayers of the saints. In other words, it seems that the literary-theological function of the verse keeps with John's style and intent. The prayers of the saints are important enough to God that there is silence in heaven, a deliberate awaiting of these prayers, and then an action in response to them. On the one hand, we pray for God's judgement and rule to come; on the other hand, *we* don't inaugurate it or consummate it. It remains *his* rule.

Note the interaction at this point between God's reigning and the saints' prayers. We can't play one off against the other. Prayer is important, even vital, and does not take place in vain. God is moved by prayer, while at the same time he is who he is, not by petition or request, but by his very nature. He has accomplished, is accomplishing, and will accomplish his will in the universe. His purposes will not be thwarted or defied. God's rule will be consummated, but this is not in exclusion to the prayers of the saints. You may be thinking, 'If there were no prayers of the saints would God's purposes be accomplished?' I would say yes, but at the same time encourage us to see that this does not seem to be the way God has set things up. As far as I can tell, prayer and God's purposes somehow fit together. The explanation of precisely 'how' all this works out will have to wait until we see Christ face to face.

THE SEVENTH SEAL & THE SIX TRUMPETS (1)

(3-5) An angel (or Christlike figure) offers the prayers of the saints, not in any mediational sense, but simply by presentation. The double imagery of both prayer and incense offered on the altar before the throne probably implies the sacrificial character of prayer (Ps. 141:2).

The smoke of the incense rises to God with the prayers. Just as incense and smoke accompanied sacrifice by God's people in the Old Testament, they now accompany the prayers of the saints in the Apocalypse. Perhaps, the connection between the two should be seen in that both are pleasing to God.

God's response to the prayers follows. From it we make the association of fire being hurled to the earth, thunder, lighting, and an earthquake as portraying God's judgement.

It is noteworthy that each time these various phenomena occur together, they occur in the setting of the temple of God or his throne. Each time they are found they mark an important event, and each time after 4:5 (where they first occur) there is an increase of the phenomena.

Here, for example, they mark the end of the opening of the seven seals. In 11:19 they mark (with the addition of the hailstorm) the end of the sounding of the seventh trumpet and in 16:18 they mark the end of the pouring out of the seven bowls of wrath, expanding the effects of the earthquake and hail.

John often repeats and deepens motifs he has already used. Each repetition shows the reader how much closer the end is, while at the same time affirming that in spite of all that's going on, for the most part, people refuse to turn to God and glorify him (9:20, 16:9-11).

God's judgement then is becoming more and more severe. It doesn't come all at once, but deepens in its intensity as history moves on. This action correlates in a remarkable manner, at least in some sense, with the prayers of the saints. Prayer is not in vain and God's reign is not diminished.

ii) 8:6-12

(6-12) And now, the seven angels prepare to sound the seven trumpets. Trumpets are richly associated with the Old Testament in four ways: 1) Trumpets frequently accompany ceremonial processions with the ark involving Israel's preparation for battle (Josh. 6; Neh. 12:41). Jericho is an example of this where the ark was accompanied by trumpeters, and at the final blast the walls of the city fell. 2) Often in the Old Testament we find trumpets blown to proclaim the accession of a king or to proclaim God as King (i.e. 1 Kings 1:34, 39; Numb. 23:21; Zech. 9:14). 3) Trumpets regularly announce an alarm or call to repentance in the face of God's judgement (i.e. Jer. 4:5, 6:1, 17; Joel 2:1, 15). 4) Trumpets were sounded at all feasts in Israel on the first day of the month and at the sacrifice given each day to remember God.

John wants his readers to realize the significance of these seven trumpets and their Old Testament associations. The call is to repentance and to remember God as the reigning King. However, if we are not convinced we can so closely associate all of these, we can at least affirm the association of these trumpets to both the reign of God as well as a call to repentance (9:20, 11:19).

It is important to note that the sounding of the first four trumpets, although affecting people, is primarily concerned with natural disasters. The devastation affects only a third of the earth and trees.

God's final judgement has not yet come. He still uses these disasters to bring people to repentance. Also noteworthy is that in the description of these first four trumpet blasts John alludes to the great Egyptian plagues.

The first trumpet sounds. Hail and fire mix with blood, recalling the seventh Egyptian plague (Ex. 9:23 ff) and also may have a background in Joel 2:30. This mixture is hurled to the earth and a third of the earth is burned up including a third of the trees and all the green grass of this scorched area.

The second trumpet sounds. This time a third of the sea is turned to blood and a third of the sea creatures die, which is reminiscent of the Nile being turned to blood causing the fish to die (Ex. 7:20 ff). Also, a third of the ships are destroyed.

The third trumpet sounds. The effects of which again recall the first Egyptian plague, this time a third of the fresh water turns bitter and people die from drinking it. The star affecting the water is called Wormwood, which may be a reference to the strong bitter-tasting plant of the same name.

The fourth trumpet sounds, recalling the ninth Egyptian plague, darkness. Again, the effect is partial.

The plagues in Egypt were intended to provoke Pharaoh to change his mind, to repent. These disasters, in the present context (9:20, 11:19), have a clear typological connection to the plagues, and function here in a similar way.

Just as Pharaoh was God's enemy in the time of the Exodus, so now 'the inhabitants of the earth' (as we've seen ample evidence of in this book) are God's enemies. They too are given an opportunity to repent. The result of the plagues sent upon Pharaoh and Egypt culminated in Israel's great deliverance, the Exodus. They were liberated from slavery and eventually brought into the Promised Land.

Could it be that these disasters are but a prelude to the great deliverance to come? Only this time, Christians are to be brought into the new heavens and the new earth forever. That is, their destiny is not to be brought into a land of milk and honey, but into the very presence of a loving God and the Lamb.

THE SEVENTH SEAL & THE SIX TRUMPETS (2) (8:1-9:21)

General Review

In chapter 8 the opening of the seventh seal brought about silence in heaven. We explored three possible explanations for this. First, the silence represented a dramatic pause as all heaven stands in awe of the impending judgements of God. The second explanation proposed that the silence reflects an absolute stillness, a return to that which existed at creation. The third explanation highlighted the prayers of the saints. These prayers are important enough to God that there is silence in heaven (verses 1-2), awaiting a sacrificial-oriented reception of these prayers and then an action related to them (verses 3-5).

In verses 7-12 the sounding of the first four trumpets and the plagues associated with them dealt primarily with natural disasters. Each time a trumpet is blown there is a partial devastation, announcing God's judgement, which is not yet here in its final all-consuming sense, but arrives at this point in a limited way. An Egyptian-Exodus typology is at work where the plagues of hail, water, blood, and darkness here are reminiscent of some of the very same plagues brought upon Egypt and Pharaoh, resulting in Israel's liberation from slavery.

As I see it, these verses may be seen from two perspectives. First, in regard to believers, the Exodus, which led to Israel's eventual entrance to the Promised Land, may have been in John's mind. He would likely, by implication at least, make the connection between his visions of the future and the historic events of the past. John's readers, familiar with the Exodus, would have also seen the bigger picture. The great liberating act in Israel's history, the Exodus, is typological. It relates to God's greatest redemptive act, that of sending his son Jesus Christ to die for the sins of the world and to be raised to life. Both these acts brought release from slavery; the first one to the Promised Land, the second, to everlasting life with God and the Lamb.

We will have to wait and see if this motif is more than implied as we go on to look at the rest of the book. It would be surprising, however, not to see God's intent in sending these types of plagues as a reminder to his persecuted people that, as Israel had been liberated from slavery in Egypt and brought into the Promised Land, the reigning Lord will also liberate them from slavery to sin and death, and bring them into his everlasting presence, regardless of how bleak their present circumstances are.

Second, in regard to unbelievers, the plagues are sent as judgements and John sees them as such. They are the consequential outpouring, albeit partially, of the wrath of God and the Lamb (6:17). The effect of these natural disasters, which no doubt also affected human beings, was partial. Why only a third? It would seem here that an Exodus typology is significant. The plagues brought upon Pharaoh and Egypt aimed to bring Pharaoh to repentance and at the same time to bring glory to God. Each time Pharaoh refused to free the Israelites another plague was sent. The typology, while not exact, is close enough for us to see the parallel. God's enemies, 'the inhabitants of the earth' in verse 13, are also given an opportunity to repent as 9:20 seems to make clear.

Although we must remember that these visions are given for the believing community, the concern includes not only the end of the story for believers, but also for unbelievers. If in fact these verses (visions) have two perspectives, that of believers as well as unbelievers, woven into an Exodus typology, what holds them together?

I believe the trumpets are the key. Remember, the rich associations with trumpets in the Old Testament point to at least two things: first, the sounding of trumpets often proclaims God's reign; second, trumpets often announce a call to repentance in the face of God's judgement. Both the proclamation and the call are associated with these visions.

iii) 8:13-9:1-21

(13) After the triple "woe" to the inhabitants of the earth, the next two trumpets sound. They deal primarily with plagues on humans. (The seventh and last trumpet is not sounded until 11:15; as with the seventh seal there is an interlude prior to the event).

(1-2) As the fifth angel sounds his trumpet, John sees a star descend from the sky to earth. In this context the star is a person. He is given a key, demonstrating his lack of authority to open the Abyss. When the Abyss (which most likely refers to a type of prison inhabited by spiritual beings that are both in rebellion against God and under his control) is opened, smoke pours forth darkening sun and sky.

(3-5) Here we again have Exodus typology, although in this context the locusts are not ordinary locusts, but locusts with power like scorpions. They are told not to harm the earth's vegetation, but only the people without the seal of God. It would seem these scorpion-like locusts are in fact imprisoned demons, now released to torture those not sealed. Notice they do not have the power to kill, only to torture for five months. It is important to note here that just as God distinguished between the Israelites and Egyptians at the time of the plagues (Ex. 8:22 ff, 9:2 ff), he is now also able to distinguish between those sealed and those subjected to the torture of the locusts.

(6) The agony of such circumstances will cause people to seek death, but they will not find it. Death will elude them. In these verses there is again the idea of a limited time of punishment in order to bring about repentance. In other words, God's wrath is still partial. The verses also show that God's enemies cannot continue to ignore his judgement.

(7-13) Reminiscent of Joel 2 and Exodus 10, John now gives us a much more elaborate description of the locusts. Their appearance is terrifying. The king over them is described as the angel of the Abyss: Abaddon in Hebrew or Apollyon in Greek, meaning destruction or destroyer. Thus with the appearance of the locusts, the first woe is passed and two more are to come. The sixth angel sounds his trumpet. From the golden altar before God, John hears a voice. This is possibly another inference to the prayers of the saints. If so, this places even more emphasis on the importance of prayer as it relates to the consummation of God's kingdom.

(14-16) Four angels are released to kill a third of humankind. This release is in accordance with God's timing right down to the hour, day, month, and year. These angels also seem as demonic as the locusts, but we are not told exactly what role they play in the devastation. John quickly shifts his attention to the two hundred million mounted troops. Perhaps, the angels themselves led these troops.

(17-19) John now gives a description of the horses, as it is they who are used to bring about the devastation. Again, we must recognize that the vision doesn't portray natural events.

These horses are no ordinary horses, but are demonically destructive. Their heads are like lions and they have fire, smoke, and sulphur coming out of their mouths. In this way John shows that the horses are somewhat similar to the locusts; both are evil and demonic.

(20-21) In spite of all these plagues, the remaining two-thirds of humanity still do not repent. As Pharaoh had refused to recognize God's reign, now too the survivors do not repent and continue in their idolatry (Ps. 115:4; Jer. 1:16).

Lamentably, yet ironically they continue to worship demons, the very beings used, under the reign of God, to bring about the plagues. They continue to produce murder, practice sorcery (which is significantly the same word used for the works of the Egyptian magicians in Ex. 7:11, 22), indulge in sexual immorality, and revel in theft.

These two chapters have given us the events surrounding the opening of the seventh seal: the silence in heaven, the remarkable significance of the prayers of the saints in relationship to the coming consummation of God's kingdom, and his final judgement is more fully in evidence.

The first four trumpets, with all the parallels of the Exodus and some of the plagues associated with it, seem to affirm the reign of God as well as a call to repentance. The last two trumpets, with the continuing Exodus typology, deal more emphatically with the judgement of humanity than the previous four.

The fifth trumpet brings anguish and torment for a limited time, while the sixth trumpet deepens the degree of judgement and death for a third of humanity. In each case, the activity is demon-centered, though not outside of God's control. The imagery is striking, revealing that God's judgement has begun and it is working its way to completion. Believers will be spared, but woe to the inhabitants of the earth!

THE LITTLE SCROLL (10:1-11)

General Review

Previously we looked in some detail at chapters 8 and 9 and the sounding of the six trumpets. The first four related primarily to natural disasters, and the second two relate more directly to the torture and human death. The typological character of the visions in these chapters and the significance of the role of trumpets are clear. Both announce God's reign and his call to repentance. The response to the unleashing of God's wrath has been, to say the least, one of complacence and hard-heartedness (9:20-21). Those that remain still do not repent at this point, neither of their false worship, nor of their sinful acts.

Introduction

In chapter 10 we move into an interlude before we get to the sounding of the seventh trumpet in 11:15.

Text

i) 10:1-7

(1) John sees a mighty angel coming down from heaven (5:2), implying John himself is back on the earth. As far back as 4:3 John was writing from a heavenly vantage point. This mighty angel is described in much the same way as God or Christ at various places throughout Scripture (Ps. 104:3; Rev. 1:16, 4:3; Ex. 13:21 ff; Dan. 12:7 ff). However, the context makes it clear that the angel is just that, an angel, a messenger from God.

(2-4) The angel John sees is holding a little scroll. In contrast to the scroll God held in 5:1, this one is open. The descending angel puts one foot on the land and the other on the sea, indicating perhaps both the authority and the breadth of his message. The shout of the angel is as a roar of a lion; something that demands attention. In response to this shout, the voices of the seven thunders speak. Thunder is usually connected with God's judgement (Ps. 29; Jn. 12:28). Are the seven thunders' voices to be associated with the judgement of God?

It seems John understood these voices and was about to write down their revelation, but is forbidden to do so by another voice from heaven. John does not give us enough information to be sure of the identities of the voices or to understand their message. Concealment may have something to do with either the significance of the message; it was too sacred to be revealed (2 Cor. 12:3-4), or its insignificance given that there is to be only one more series of sevens before the end, that of the bowls of wrath in chapter 16. This latter possibility may be affirmed in the following verses, but it is difficult to precisely ascertain how all this should be understood.

(5-7) It soon becomes clear that the next steps in the process of God's unfolding wrath will take place without delay (12:7). The angel swears an oath in the name of the One who has created the universe, the everlasting God. It is only he who is able to bring an end to history and who is able to carry out his promises and purposes.

This may relate to both an assurance for the persecuted church and the sealing of the seven thunders. Recall the way of the martyrs in 6:9-11 (be patient), and the response, if we have understood 8:3-5 correctly, to the prayers of the saints in bringing about the consummation of God's rule and final judgement. There in chapter 8, each time a trumpet sounds, partial devastation occurs. Here in chapter 10, it seems that we have moved from the 'not yet, be patient' or 'partial judgement' to the assured consummation of the rule of God, bringing both blessings to those who believe and destruction to those who do not.

The angel is even more specific with a strong adversative, "but in the days," while at the same time not precise about the timing of the sounding of the seventh trumpet. This would seem to imply a period of time directly related to this last trumpet in 11:15, the seven bowls of chapter 16, and the consummation of God's rule in chapters 20-22. After 11:15 and the sounding of the seventh trumpet, there is no turning back. During this period of time the 'mystery of God,' probably referring to his whole purpose of salvation and the defeat of evil, will be accomplished just as God has announced it to his servants the prophets, and through Christ, to John himself.

ii) 10:8-11

(8-10) John is instructed to go and take the open scroll from the angel standing on the land and the sea and eat it. It will turn his stomach sour, but be as sweet as honey in his mouth. What is going on here? Certainly Ezekiel 2:8-3:4 provides a parallel to our text and is worth consulting for the similar imagery which in establishes Ezekiel's call as prophet. The symmetry between the two passages illustrates that John's vision is connected to other prophets who had preceded him. Yet it leaves us with several unanswered questions. Why would the scroll be as sweet as honey in John's mouth, yet turn his stomach sour (Ps. 119:103; Jer. 15:16; Ezk. 3:1-4)? Does it have anything to do with the contents of the scroll? Perhaps, the sweetness and bitterness relates to the prophetic call and commissioning of John, which at this point is being renewed in light of the seriousness of what is about to be revealed. I believe the context of chapter 10 will help us discover at least responses to these questions.

In spite of the fact that John gives us little go on it is important to try to discern the contents of the scroll. Some understand the contents as a description of what takes place in 11:1-13 as a message to the church. Believers will experience opposition, even death, at the hands of Satan and the enemies of God. The scroll is sweet-tasting because it is the word of God, but it also turns John's stomach sour because of the persecution believers must go through. This view may be moving along the right lines, but is it satisfactory? Verse 11 seems to hint that the contents of the scroll have a wider scope than just that of the church. The commission to prophesy, which immediately follows the ingestion of the scroll, indicates a relationship of its contents to John's calling.

Others understand the contents of the scroll to be the coming judgements for unbelievers, the wrath of God reaching its climax. Its sweetness again comes from the fact that the scroll is the word of God, but according to this view John's stomach turns sour because of the awfulness of the judgement coming upon the world.

Another possibility is to take the two previous views together. Their related emphasis on the sweetness of the word of God and their distinct emphasis on John's stomach turning sour compliment each other. The word of God is sweet to the prophet and God's people, but it turns the prophet's stomach sour in the following way.

The message of the scroll will be sweet or sour depending on when and to whom it is delivered. The scroll is sweet for the believer and unbeliever concerning God's grace, his plan for history, and his desire that all would repent, but also bitter for believers concerning their persecution and death, and for unbelievers in that God's wrath is coming upon them.

There is one more possibility. Perhaps, the contents of the scroll relate primarily to the prophet and his task; they are the commission and command to prophesy. In other words, the whole scene is to be understood as an Ezekiel-type of prophetic call-narrative that heightens the seriousness of the times. The reception of the word of God is like honey in the prophet's mouth, but as the prophet realizes that his vocation, as the Old Testament prophets before him, will consist largely in a rejection of his mission and message, his stomach turns bitter.

(11) John's mission includes a command to prophesy. The days of the seventh trumpet are about to begin. God's wrath will no longer be constrained, and his redemptive activity in Christ will culminate in the consummation of his rule and the new heavens and new earth.

TWO WITNESSES & THE SEVENTH TRUMPET (11:1-19)

General Review

Our conclusion, at the end of chapter 10, was that there was little information available about the seven thunders and the message given through them. In verses 5-7 John sees an angel vowing that there will be no further delay. The sounding of the seventh trumpet will bring an end to the end, and God's whole purpose of salvation and all that it involves will be accomplished. We also discussed the scroll in verses 8-10 and why it is described as sweet as honey in John's mouth yet sour in his stomach, suggesting a few possibilities concerning the scroll's contents, noting that John himself offers us very few answers.

Concerning the scroll, note that the following four interpretations were offered: first, the scroll's message to the church is sweet-tasting as the word of God, but caused the prophet's stomach to sour because of the ongoing and coming persecution facing believers. Second, the scroll is a message to unbelievers for the wrath of God now reaches its climax; again, sweet as the word of God, but sour because of the awful judgements coming on the world. Third, the scroll is a combination of these two. Sweet is the word of God, though its message is sour to both believers and unbelievers. Fourth, the eating of the scroll affirms John's commission and the command to prophesy. Again, it is sweet as the word of God in its message of judgement and salvation, and it is sour because the prophet realizes that his vocation, similar to the Old Testament prophets before him, will bring with it a rejection of his mission and message. This is a prophetic call-narrative.

All four explanations are within the realm of possibility. There may be others, but we are constrained by the text itself in following two directions. We should not be too dogmatic when it comes to the contents of the scroll, but neither should we align ourselves with just any interpretation. We simply don't have enough information for complete clarity, but there is a domain of meaning that allows something relevant about the text to emerge. Possibly all four of these in some specific way fit the context. After all, the contents deal with believers and unbelievers while also affirming that, as a prophet, John is commissioned by God.

Introduction

This chapter is notoriously difficult to interpret, and much depends on how much of it we understand to be symbolic. Remember, apocalyptic literature is not historical narrative. In pointing this out, I certainly am not intending to say that because language is figurative or symbolic it is not historical. Symbolism or non-symbolism does not mean historicity or non-historicity, truth or non-truth. This kind of either-or reasoning is more modernist in orientation, than it is truly biblical. We must try, even though we cannot do this perfectly, to adopt our criteria from what God has revealed. Imposing our own criteria on Scripture tends to shape it towards our own ends, and when this takes place we are more likely than not to miss God's precious message as revealed in the biblical accounts. In this case, God is using a highly symbolic form of literature in aiming to communicate his message concerning the end of history which will take place, though it may not happen exactly as we suppose.

There are at least three possible ways of interpreting the language in these passages. The first is literal; the second and third are more symbolic. The first view is dispensational. I will not deal with this interpretative possibility in the text section of the exposition as I find it a less likely option than one of the two which follow. The dispensational interpretation posits that John's prophecy speaks of a literal-historical restoration of the Jewish temple in Jerusalem prior to the end of the age and the conflict between the restored Jews and the antichrist (the beast). Remember, according to this view Christians are raptured in 4:1. This older dispensational view has recently been modified by at least one of its major defenders who argues for the same interpretation, while advocating a more 'symbolic language' approach to the section.

The next two interpretations posit these verses are purely symbolic. The first view considers this section to be prophecy for the church in regards to the oppression and persecution it will face in the last days. John's prophecy refers to believers facing the horrendous circumstances of living in an unbelieving world; however, the good news is that God is reigning and those who are his need not fear. Within this first symbolic option there are several nuances which we will focus on later.

The second symbolic interpretation responds to the question about what was going to happen to God's ancient people, the Jews, in the last days. This section is thought to be similar in content to Romans 9-11 where Paul speaks of the eventual salvation of all Israel. Israel in Romans 11:25-32 is assumed by some to be the Jews, physical-national Israel. This position argues for a similar understanding here. The revelation to John in this chapter concerns the Jews in the last days.

Let's look at the text considering the first symbolic view, which understands these verses as concerning the church.

Text

i) 11:1-14 The Two Witnesses

First Symbolic View

(**1-2**) John, raised a Jew and familiar with the symbolism of the temple, is told to measure the temple of God, the altar, and the worshipers. In the Old Testament, measuring can be for destruction or preservation (Ezk. 40-42; 2 Sam. 8:12). In our context, measurements are taken as a protection of the church. In the New Testament the phrase 'temple of God' is used frequently to symbolize the church (1 Cor. 3:16-17; 2 Cor. 6:6; Eph. 2:16-22). God will give, as we have seen before, not protection from persecution and martyrdom, but ultimate protection from his impending wrath. The outer court of the temple has been given to the Gentiles, so it is not to be measured. Again, this may reference the church, but from another angle. From this perspective, the outer court given to the Gentiles refers to the persecution the church will face and the limited time (forty-two months) in which she is to face it. (Another view states the outer court is simply for unbelievers, not measured and therefore not protected).

Unbelieving Gentiles will trample the holy city for a period of forty-two months. Here, the holy city is a reference to the church. Those who persecute the church will be able to do so only for a limited period of time and although the church will face oppression, it will not be destroyed. The limited time frame is reminiscent of the time when Antiochus Epiphanes, in the book of Daniel, inflicted great suffering on the Jews.

(3-4) In these verses the two witnesses are granted power for their mission (1:2, 19:10). They will prophesy, meaning they will witness to the Lordship of Jesus Christ and call for repentance.

The identity of these two witnesses is highly debated, with usually at least ten to twelve possibilities offered. The particular view we are dealing with at the moment understands these two witnesses as representative of the church. In other words, these two witnesses, similar to Moses and Elijah in the Old Testament, are not individuals but symbolic of the church and its witness in the last days (notice also a necessity for the two witnesses to gain adequate testimony Dt. 17:16, 19:15; Jn. 8:17). The time period for the two witnesses to prophecy is 1,260 days, the same period of time the holy city or church will face devastation but not destruction. This is the same period of time which the antichrist is given power and authority (13:5-8).

The understanding that the two witnesses are the church is affirmed in verse 4. They are symbolized by the two olive trees and they witness by the Spirit of God (Zech. 4:3 ff). Remember, in chapter 1 John referred to seven lampstands as the seven churches. Some correlate this with the whole church, but others say that because there are only two lampstands and not more, this means that only part of the church is meant; the part to be martyred.

(5-6) Protection is offered and unusual powers are given to the witnesses. These capacities are similar to those of Elijah (1 Kings 18:24, 38; 2 Kings 10-12) and Moses (Ex. 7:20, 8:12). This affirms that just as Moses and Elijah had unique abilities, so now the church during these 1,260 days will be equipped to carry out its task of witnessing for God.

(7-10) Once the testimony of the witnesses is accomplished, they will be killed by the beast which came out of the Abyss, a possible reference to the antichrist (Dan. 7:21). The bodies of the witnesses lie in the street of the great city, which most likely is Rome, not Jerusalem, on the basis that at least seven times in this book 'great city' or 'Babylon the great' is used symbolically to refer to Rome (14:8, 16:19, 17:18, 18:2, 10, 16, 18).

At the time of John's writing, Rome was known by Christians to be both wicked and oppressive. John figuratively refers to the city as Sodom and Egypt to highlight its anti-God character. The end of verse 8, "where also their Lord was crucified" broadens (by way of Jerusalem, being under control of the Romans) the previous statement concerning Rome to include the whole of humanity in defiance and rebellion against God. The witnesses are refused burial, an outrage and the ultimate insult in the ancient world. The fact that humanity will see them reinforces the broadening of verse 8 to include all those who stand against God. The inhabitants of the earth, a phrase repeatedly used in this book to describe those who insist on being enemies of God, have a party to rejoice in the fact that those who once tormented them are now dead. Just like the witnesses, God's revelation through the prophets has always confronted and challenged those opposed to him.

This should cause us to ask ourselves, 'Have I tormented anyone recently with the truth of God's word? Have I become too comfortable and complacent in an increasingly evil world?' These are truly important questions to ponder!

(11) The apparent victory over the witnesses of God is short-lived. After the three and a half days, the breath of life from God enters the witnesses and they stand once again as living beings. Similarly, in Ezekiel the Jewish nation is likened to scattered bones. The bones are brought together clothed with flesh, and God breathes into them and they live. In reaction to both of these events, the enemies of God are struck with terror.

(12-14) After being brought to life, the witnesses are raised to heaven. This does not take place secretly, but before the eyes of their enemies. As this happens there is a terrible earthquake, killing seven thousand and causing a tenth of the great city to be destroyed. Some suggest the survivors give glory to God and repent. Others would argue the survivors give glory to God only out of fear and terror. The phrase here does not speak of a change of heart, but of a forced acknowledgement.

Second Symbolic View

We now turn to consider the implications of the second symbolic point of view. According to this view our text is similar to what Paul writes in Romans 9-11, and concerns God's people, the Jews, in the last days. This perspective shares some features with the first symbolic view so it won't be treated in as much detail. However, this does not mean it is a less viable interpretation.

(1-2) These verses also refer to protection from God's wrath but in contrast the worshippers in the temple are a faithful remnant of Jews. The inner court of the temple was strictly for Jews; it is now measured off, protected, and separated in an even greater way from the outer court of the Gentiles. There is a distinction between those measured as the true worshippers, the faithful Jewish Christians in the holy city, and the Gentiles. This view argues that the holy city must be Jerusalem, representative of the nation of Israel. Both the Gentiles and the holy city symbolize the non-Christian. In this case, we have an affirmation of God's faithfulness to his people, the Jews. He has not cast them off, but has kept a remnant to himself, which he consistently does in the Old Testament, through whom he will eventually bring the whole nation (Ezk. 14:22; Rom. 11:4). Like the previous view, the forty-two months speak of a limited time of repression, however the holy city is not the church but Jerusalem itself, a representative of the nation of Israel in its rejection of God.

(3-5) Even though the holy city has been trampled by unbelievers, God has not given up on his people. He will send two witnesses to them to prophesy. According to this view, it is better to see these two witnesses as two individuals, rather than the church, given the details in the text about the character and description of their mission. They are two witnesses sent to Israel to bring conversion. As we saw in verse 4, the olive trees and lampstands are reminiscent of the vision given to Zechariah. This imagery is used to affirm the witnesses are sent by God and authorized by him to convert the Jews on his behalf. Verse 5 affirms the fact that the witnesses will not come to harm for the moment. The identity of the witnesses is thought to be connected to the mission of Elijah, Moses, mentioned previously, or Jeremiah (Jer. 5:14).

(6-8) The connection to Elijah, Moses, and Jeremiah may hint to the identity of the witnesses. Elijah was given the power to stop the rain, Moses the power over the waters and plagues (Ex. 7:20; 1 Kings 17:1; Lk. 4:25; Jas. 5:17), and God made the words in Jeremiah's mouth a fire that would consume his rebellious people.

This second interpretation does not argue for a literal return of the two witnesses, but rather envisions the two individuals as having a similar function as Elijah, Moses, and Jeremiah. They are two historical persons who will come with God's message to rebellious Israel in the last days.

In verse 7, after the testimony is accomplished, the beast or antichrist kills the two prophets. In verse 8, the bodies lie in the street of the great city, probably Jerusalem. However, Jerusalem is not symbolic for the whole nation of Israel. But because of the mention of "where the Lord was crucified," it should be taken literally as Jerusalem. In other words, this view argues that the actual city of Jerusalem will have a role in the unfolding of the last days.

(9-12) As the prophets are killed, the entire world, including Jerusalem, looks on. The two prophets are refused burial and the enemies of God rejoice in the death of their tormentors. However, the story is not over. The resurrection of the prophets in verse 11, it is argued, will bring about the conversion of Israel. To take this as an intended assurance for the church in the midst of persecution misses the fact that terror struck those who saw it. The prophets' ascension in verse 12 again affirms to their enemies that they were truly prophets empowered and commissioned by God.

(13) A tenth of the city of Jerusalem is now destroyed and seven thousand are dead (perhaps including non-Jews). The rest, those who give glory to God, are literally Jews. Therefore, verse 13 relates to all of Israel. Because of God's acts at the end of history, all Israel will come to know Christ and repent, thereby giving glory to God in heaven.

ii) 11:14-19 The Seventh Trumpet

(14-15) The unfolding drama in the opening of the seventh seal resulted in heaven's silence. In contrast, as the seventh trumpet is sounded there are loud voices in heaven. These moments bring us to the height of suspense, but the end is not yet complete. However, there is now a new and marked difference. The loud voices pronounce that the kingdom of the world has become the kingdom of our Lord and of his Christ who will reign forever and ever. God's rule now openly takes its rightful place as the seventh trumpet sounds. It is in this period of time that the end will come. This final episode will bring with it the assurance that God is reigning. Those who are his need not fear. God's reign is ultimate. There is no authority in all of heaven or earth greater than his.

(16-17) The acknowledgement of God's ultimate reign is seen as the twenty-four elders (4:10, 7:11) fall and worship God, proclaiming his power and authority. He is the One who was and is. Note that 'who is to come' is left out. God's visitation is now. The consummation of the kingdom of God is at hand. The response to the prayer, "Your kingdom come, your will be done," is actively and dynamically taking place before our eyes and God's mighty rule is no longer only for those with eyes of faith, but now is visibly established by the destruction of all rebellion. This does not mean that at some point of time in history God was not reigning. The point is God will now reign exclusively and completely. There will be no more counterfeit powers; there will be no more evil, no more sin or death. God's great power can defeat and overpower all his enemies in the final conflict.

(18-19) The nations that defy God are his true enemies. In reference to them, God's wrath is unleashed. However, because God's grace was made manifest in the blood of the Lamb, believers are protected from this wrath. The time has arrived for judging, rewarding, and destroying. These two realities, reward and destruction, will be fleshed out in relationship to judgement as we move into chapter 20. In other words, there will be much more to say in reference to the judgement of the dead as it relates to reward and destruction.

Verse 19 corresponds to this idea of reward and destruction in two ways. First, the temple is opened and the Ark of the Covenant seen. In the Old Testament the ark was a symbol of God's presence with his people. There is no greater reward than to be in his presence. Second, there is lightening, thunder, earthquakes, and hail. We have pointed out previously, the relationship of these various different types of cosmic, earthly phenomena usually symbolizes God's wrath. The assurance that God has faithfully carried out his covenant promises should comfort his people. He will reward them by drawing near to them.

THE WOMAN, HER SON & THE DRAGON (12:1-17)

Introduction

Chapters 12, 13, and 14 give a series of visions related to one of the central themes in the book. The visions are primarily concerned with the terrible persecution the churches will face for their faith. The goal is to communicate to them God's victory over Satan who has opposed the Christ and sought to destroy him. Satan's power is very real, as evidenced in the persecution and martyrdom of God's people. However, God's triumph is also sure. The salvific victory accomplished by the Lamb is efficacious and everlasting.

Text

i) 12:1-6

(1-2) The vision begins here with a great and wondrous sign

appearing in the sky. No explanation is given as to the origin of the sign, nor are we given any hint of how to decode the imagery. As a result of this ambiguity, there are several ways this chapter is interpreted.

Many have thought, for example, the woman mentioned is literally Mary, the mother of Jesus. If so, this would be an unlikely description as Mary is too specific a character for such symbolism. Others who interpret this part of the verse symbolically posit the woman, clothed in the sun, represents the heavenly church arrayed in splendor and majesty (Isa. 7:10, 26:17, 54:1, 66). For this view, the idea that this is an actual historical woman does not seem to be consistent with John's symbolism throughout Revelation. If this is the case, the descriptions in this chapter are not predictions of historical events, but pictures intending to represent the battle between God and Satan, which has historical effects. The heavenly conflict has an earthly counterpart as the battle between the church as God's people and Satan and his demonic forces is waged. As we proceed to look at the rest of the chapter the details of how this possible interpretation works itself out become clear. We will call this the "S" view because it holds that the images are entirely symbolic.

Before we go on to that perspective, there are two other possible interpretations of the woman in labor that need to be considered. The first interpretation argues that the imagery references the Old Testament (Isa. 26:17, 54:1). It is possible to understand the woman in labor representing Israel, Jerusalem, or Zion. She is the mother of the people of God. Instead of being completely symbolic, this view weaves together symbolic and literal interpretations at different points in reference to John's typological echoes of the Old Testament, which will be explained further as we go on. We will call this the "SL" view. The SL view emphasizes the fact that Old Testament Israel failed to bring about salvation. This salvation can only be accomplished by the Messiah whose birth is about to take place through Israel.

The second potential interpretation (considering both Old Testament and New Testament imagery in verses 1-2) argues the woman is the earthly church. This does not mean there is not a heavenly church, but that the woman is primarily symbolic of the disciples (who are the church) based on John 16:19-22. The pain and sadness she experiences through labor represents the Passion of Christ; the joy that follows in birth represents the resurrection. In this context where the woman represents Christ's disciples (note the twelve stars), it is the disciples (the earthly church) who cry out in pain. The pain is from the Passion as they participate in the sufferings of the Messiah, and it is also they who are about to give birth to the church because of the resurrection. This is not to be thought of as the origin of the resurrection, but the transmission of the truth of the resurrection, which in turn gives birth to the church. We will call this the symbolic, literal, and existential, or "SLE" view. We will repeatedly return to these three possibilities as we study this chapter.

(3-4a) Following the woman in labor, John mentions another sign in the sky. The dragon, a familiar figure of evil in Scripture, now enters the scene. He is red, with seven heads, seven crowns and ten horns. Again, it is important to remember the significance of typology for the Apocalypse. There is much in this book associated with the Exodus. Pharaoh, for example, was himself called a dragon (Ezk. 29:3, 32:2), and Egypt often represents evil especially in reference to its persecution of God's people. Satan is presented as one with great power and authority. The heads, horns, and crowns, along with the ability to fling stars to earth, all speak of the might and strength of evil and subsequently, the evil one.

(4b-5) Here the child, a male, is born. Satan takes his position to devour him. This is his ultimate purpose. In interpreting these events we refer to our three interpretive possibilities:

The S view argues there is no need to reference a specific event in the birth of the child as if this is a literal reference to Jesus' birth by Mary. The aim, according to the S view, is to symbolize the age-old hostility of Satan to God's Messiah. Arguably, if this was intended to be literal, it is strange that there is no mention of the cross. This view concludes that the "b" part of verse 5 can hardly be referring to the ascension of Christ as this is never thought of as being an escape from Satan. The Christ does not escape Satan, but confronts him and triumphs over him by the cross and the resurrection. The point here John wishes to emphasize is that this triumph has already been accomplished and has repercussions for the future.

The SL view contends the protection of the child from the dragon is a reference to God's protecting the Incarnate Son who is to have authority and dominion. John's objective is to show how the incarnation is to be an encouragement to believers.

The emphasis here is on the ascension and the concern is the church. Just as God protected his Son through suffering and death, so will he protect his people from spiritual death and destruction. Believers should be confident of God's ageless purpose.

The SLE view does not consider these verses as a reference to the birth of the Messiah, but to his resurrection. This perspective is based on John 16:19-22. The twelve disciples as the new community of God's people are like a woman in the pain of childbirth. After the resurrection, this community rejoices as a woman who gives birth to a child.

The first community of believers in Christ could be seen as the mother of the resurrected Christ, not in the sense that she is the origin of his resurrection, but in the sense that witness to the resurrected Christ passes through the community's existential experience, aiming to show its importance for the forming of the church. These verses deal with the resurrection of Christ and his ascension and their significance for the church.

(6) According to the S view this passage is not a historic account of

Christians escaping at the time of the Jewish war of 70 CE, as some may have it. More likely it is a reference to the dragon turning on the heavenly church after his failure to destroy the Messiah.

The point here is God's faithfulness to protect the woman in the last days of Satan's assault. By interpreting these images as symbolic, we can say with certainty that God will protect his church on earth and preserve it in spite of any and all of Satan's desperately evil attempts to destroy it.

The SL understanding points out that God's people have often been in flight. The emphasis should not be on the flight, but on the fact that God faithfully protects and provides for his people. The 1,260 days (11:2, 13:5) corresponds to the time the church will face persecution and is an assurance that it will be taken care of during that time regardless of how severe or grave persecution may be.

As you may have noticed, there has been a slight shift in this position. The woman, said to be Israel in verses 1-2, now becomes the church, but the SL view argues this is not problematic for its position as apocalyptic imagery is frequently used and applied in varied ways in the same context (in verses 1-2 the woman represents Israel; in verse 6 the woman represents the church in the last days).

The SLE view presents the possibility that the reference in verse 6 is to the church during the last days. Here, the church is divinely protected and satanically persecuted for 1,260 days, but God will ultimately preserve and care for his people by providing them with refuge.

ii) 12:7-12

(7-9) The conflict between good and evil causes a war in heaven. Michael, the great archangel, protector of Israel (Dan. 7:21, 10:13, 21) and his heavenly angels fight against the dragon and his demonic angels and are victorious. Satan is, in effect, banished from any further access to God (Job 1:6ff, 2:1ff). The dragon, the ancient serpent Satan, the devil, the one who leads the whole world astray, is cast down to the earth with his angels.

Again it is important to look briefly at our three views in conjunction with these new visions. The S view contends these events are typical apocalyptic language describing a spiritual fact. In other words, this heavenly battle does not literally take place and is not an explanation of Satan's fall. John's aim is to show Satan as defeated. This, as we all know, was through the cross, not through a war of angels. The description of war is further assurance that Satan is defeated.

From the SL perspective, these verses point to the bigger picture of earthly conflicts. The battle is not just between Satan and humans, but also between angelic forces, making it a spiritual battle. This is a picture of good against evil on a universal scale.

According to the SLE argument, this defeat in battle is affirmation that Satan is no longer who he once was. His power is greatly diminished by the resurrection and ascension. He is restrained to the domain of the earth. The resurrection has brought his imminent defeat.

(10-12) Satan's defeat is another proclamation of the arrival of the rule of God and the authority of his Christ. Satan can no longer accuse as he has been barred access to God and has been partially defeated. It is by the blood of the Lamb that Christians, especially martyrs (5:9-10), have and will overcome him. The word of their testimony bears witness to this truth. Because of Christ's victory and Satan's defeat, the heavens and all who dwell in them are to rejoice. This includes Christians who remain on earth, but are citizens of heaven (Phil. 3:10). Satan however, even though overthrown, is not yet destroyed. He still has the capacity to persecute God's people and bring destruction, though his time to rule on earth is limited and his power diminished.

iii) 12:13-17

(13-17) After the heavenly battle events are repeated on the earth of some of the things already seen in heaven. According to the S view, the flight or rescue of the woman is intended to be historical. The woman symbolizes the heavenly church whom Satan continues to pursue. Satan will do anything to destroy God's people, but will not succeed. This perspective argues that the offspring of the woman are Christians who make up the church on earth, those who obey the commandments and witness to Jesus. Satan, frustrated in his attempt to destroy the heavenly woman (the church) and the Messiah, turns in his anger to the church on earth.

Conversely, the SL interpretation holds that these verses aim to show how Satan's hostility towards God's people now develops. The woman, first representing Israel in verses 1, 2, 5, and then the church in verse 6, once again becomes the church in these verses. Satan is powerless to destroy the church, but he can vent his rage on individual persons who make it up.

Likewise, the SLE position affirms these verses as referring to the church and Satan's efforts to destroy it. This view agrees that the church will be preserved during this period of fierce persecution. The emphasis is on the 'rest of her seed or offspring.' The church will not be destroyed, but its offspring produced by the disciples can be subjected to Satan's attacks.

Where does all this leave us? Let's conclude with several remarks. First, chapter 12 is steeped in Old Testament language and typology. There is much here from Egypt and the Exodus in verses 4, 6, 14, 15, 16. We see images of Pharaoh and the dragon, sustenance in the desert (Ex. 16), and the idea of wings of an eagle bringing one out of danger and into safety (Ex. 19:4). The earth even serves the people by swallowing up the enemy. There may also be an echo of Pharaoh's army in pursuit of God's people at the time of the Exodus in the image of the water spewed out of the serpent's mouth. Genesis 3:15 resonates in the reference to the "rest of her offspring or seed," emphasizing the hostility between the woman and her seed and the serpent and his. But what is the purpose of all this imagery? What historical and theological truths should it lead us to? The answer seems to lie in the truth that God is *reigning*. As shown throughout history, he is faithful to his people and will ultimately protect his own in spite of persecution or even physical death.

Second, it appears that this chapter is concerned with expressing things as they are, focusing on the here and now. Allusions to past historical events are woven into the present and the future to give the seven churches John was writing an affirmation of what God is doing in the present and how eventually the complexities of the spiritual and earthly battle that rages will be worked out. In short, God has been, is being, and will be victorious. Satan has been, is being, and will be defeated.

Third, God's consummated rule is coming soon. It has not yet completely arrived. Evil persists. Satan roves around like a roaring lion seeking to destroy those he can, seeking to blind them from the truth of heaven and earth. Praise be to God, Satan's time is limited! Praise be to God that he has provided a way for us to overcome through the blood of the Lamb.

In conclusion, whether the chapter is taken literally or not, there is and will be a historic-theological correspondence with the symbolic imagery used. Truth can be expressed in a variety of ways and we are probably wise not to be too dogmatic as to the way it is expressed here.

TWO BEASTS (13:1-18)

Introduction

Chapter 13 is a continuation of the scene in chapter 12. It opens with the image of Satan now standing on the edge of the sea calling for the first beast, who happens to be directly related to the dragon of chapter 12. This beast has ten horns, seven heads with horns, and ten crowns on each horn. He has been given power and authority by the dragon, but this power is temporary, lasting only forty-two months.

The beast makes war against Christians, which is interesting considering how this beast is related to Christ. The beast has ten crowns; Christ has many. The beast has a blasphemous name; Christ has a worthy one. The beast causes men to worship Satan; Christ calls people to worship God. The beast is wounded unto death, but is healed, showing the deliberate intention of the beast to mimic the death and Christ's resurrection. The beast has the power, authority, and throne of the dragon; Christ shares the power, authority, and throne of God. The beast's apparent death is highlighted in verse 3 where we find similar words as in 5:6, "The lamb looking as if it had been slain." 'Had been slain' is the same as the NIV translation 'fatal wound' here. Finally, we note in 5:9 that Christ redeems people from every tribe, language, people, and nation; the beast exercises authority over the people of the earth.

The beast is portrayed as a counterfeit Christ. He is the christ of Satan, the antichrist. As the dragon, Satan seeks to take God's place and to be recognized as God. The beast is his accomplice in this attempt to destroy God, and to mimic his authority, power, and work of salvation. This impersonation is the ultimate evil, claiming the work of God as the work of the devil (Mark 3:22-30). Satan and his agent are presented here as claiming to do the work of God, but in actuality are doing the work of Satan. The recognized authority of the dragon and the beast over the earth should shake us to our senses. It should make us uneasy, aware, and perhaps frightened, probing us to ask a series of questions: Do we really know the end of the story? Who will truly be victorious? Who in the end is more powerful, Christ or the beast? The beast's power is great! Who is like him? Who can make war against him? Here we wait in eager anticipation for further revelation from John concerning the denouement.

Text

i) 13:1-10

(1-2) The imagery John uses to describe the beast is associated with Daniel 7, though it seems John's primary concern is not to emulate the precision of the imagery (for example, there is only one beast compared to Daniel's four), but to capture the horror of the beast. Despite this difference in details the dragon—Satan gives the beast his power, throne, and authority. This leaves the reader wondering about the identity of the beast.

As to the identity of the beast, the most likely answer John gives is the Roman Empire. However, to limit our answer to this would cause us to miss the fact that the beast is presented as the antichrist and is therefore greater than simply the Roman Empire. Continuing with the past-present-future framework of the text that has already been established, we can say with a degree of confidence that the Empire was a foretaste of the power and authority of the beast and the dragon, but not its final manifestation.

(3) We find the beast mortally wounded, only to be restored. It is probably best to understand this as a reference to the beast itself rather than one of the Roman Emperors. For example, some would argue that this passage refers to Nero who died and was rumoured to be brought back to life. In other words, what may appear to be destroyed is not. The antichrist lives in whatever personal, power structure, or institutional forms it may take. Whether embodied as Nero or the Roman Empire, the antichrist will not be eliminated until the end. In the meantime the whole world will follow him.

(4) Not only will the beast have a following, he and the dragon will be worshiped. The question of the identity of the beast is reminiscent of several Old Testament passages concerning God (Ex. 15:11; Dt. 3:24). In each of these there is a comparison of the true God with false ones, counterfeits or idols. The question raised, "Who is like the beast?" is actually an attempt to displace God from his deserved and rightful place of incomparability.

The next question, "Who can make war against him?" brings out more clearly the political power-structure character of the previous question. Power and invincibility are attributed to the beast, a likely depiction of the Roman Empire in John's day. However, as mentioned previously, the reference should not be limited to this depiction.

(5) Note how John repeats the phrase 'was given' four times in these three verses. The use of this verb affirms that neither the beast nor the dragon is the supreme authority, but it is God who permits what is taking place to take place. Notice that he does so only for a limited period of time. The beast and the dragon, powerful as they are, are only permitted to have authority within the time-frame set by God. The words of grandeur probably refer to self-deification, and are allowed to go on for forty-two months. Although God is allowing the severe persecution of his people, ultimately he is protecting them in the midst of catastrophe.

(6) As part of his self-deification, the beast desecrates the name of God, the tabernacle, and those who live in heaven. Here again there is assurance for believers in a horrific situation. Look back to 7:15. The great multitude is in heaven before the throne of God and he who sits on the throne will spread his tabernacle over them. Read 7:16-17 and notice the themes of protection, assurance, and finality.

(7) Here, the beast is given power to make war against the saints and conquer them. It is important to notice this goes past any particular individual or state authority up to this point in history. Be it Antiochus Epiphanes in the book of Daniel; Nero, Domitian, or the Roman Empire in the Apocalypse; Lenin, Stalin, Hitler or Mao in our own day, no one person or government has yet been 'given' such great authority.

The authority of the beast extends to all the earth, portraying again the facade of victory. However, it is the saints who have the victory as evidenced in 12:11 and 15:2. Death is not the end of their story. The story ends with the blood of the Lamb and the almighty power, grace, and holiness of God. This ending challenges us to consider how this picture affects our concrete everyday existence. Does it worry or scare you? Make you angry or inspire you? If so, to do what? If not, why not? Be challenged to consider what is important in life.

(8) John repeatedly uses the phrase, "All the inhabitants of the earth" to refer to unbelievers. In verse 8 they will worship the beast. Their names are not written in the Lamb's book of life. Whether or not one is in this book depends on their relationship to him. God's everlasting plan of salvation was in Christ from the very beginning.

(9-10) This same exhortation appears at the end of the letters to the seven churches in 2:1-3:22. Verse 10 is translated in different ways because of textual variants. Some interpreters say both parts are directed to the persecutors (AV); others depict this as directed to the persecuted (NIV). There may be something here of both. It is also possible that the first half is to the persecuted—they may indeed go into exile or captivity as John himself did—and the second to the persecutors; it is they who will die by their own violent means. Both of these events call for steadfastness and faith on the part of the saints. Though they may face dire consequences, ultimate victory is theirs (14:12).

ii) 13:11-18

(11) The second beast in this chapter comes out of the earth. This beast is also presented as a counterfeit Christ, but not to the same degree as the first beast. He is less important, but his power and his aims are disgustingly evil.

(12) We know this beast's reason for being is to serve the first beast, causing the whole world to worship he whose mortal wound had been healed, but there are still unresolved questions about the identity of the second beast. The second beast aims to deceive people, probably not so much through political power as the first beast, but through mainly religious means. It seems fitting to see the imperial cult in operation here. Remember, the frequent references to the strength and demands of the imperial cult in the seven letters (2:1-3:22). Because many of its high priests occupied powerful positions in provincial and state government, the cult exercised tremendous social pressure. However, we should not limit the reference exclusively to the imperial cult, but view it as the depiction of the second beast, or as it were, the false prophet (16:13, 19:20) in John's own day.

(13) This beast is not only representative of the imperial cult, but is able to perform miraculous signs. For example, the beast causes fire to come down from heaven in an attempt to mimic God and his miracles (2 Kings 1:12).

(14) Because of these various signs, the second beast was able to deceive unbelievers. It is again significant that his power 'was given,' not possessed. The beast orders an image to be set up to honor the first beast who was fatally wounded, yet lived. This image is another allusion to resurrection, albeit one that leads the world astray. How ironic and utterly pitiful that Christ's resurrection is termed a lie or madness, while the beast's results in the world's worship. A bold attempt is being made to turn God's true activity and victory into nothing more than a mere tool in the hands of evil. No blasphemy is greater!

(15) The second beast is 'given power' to give breath and life to the image of the first beast so it can speak. Speaking icons are well attested to in the ancient world and there is little reason to think that this kind of thing, which took place through incantation or sorcery, did not happen or cannot happen again. All who don't worship the image will be killed.

(16-17) The beast obliges all, regardless of social status to receive his mark in another direct play of deception. One of the traits of the mark of the beast is its socio-economic angle; no one can buy or sell without the mark.

Should this be taken literally? How close are we to something like this becoming a reality? Technology today and in the future will enable those who use it to require encoded body marks for financial transactions. As I said previously, the second beast's deception is primarily, but not exclusively religious. Remember, it is believers who have received the mark in 7:3 (and as evidenced in 9:4) of belonging to God and therefore receiving protection from the outpouring of his wrath. We therefore have two groups of marked people. The marks show allegiance, identity, and the eventual destiny of their bearers.

(18) This particular verse calls for wisdom. While there are a preponderance of options and solutions for the number 666, none of them are conclusive. If you are interested in pursuing this verse further, I suggest you consult one of the resources listed in the bibliography.

VINDICATION & JUDGEMENT (14:1-20)

General Review

As we observed the counterfeiting activity of the two beasts in chapter 13, it became clear they are blaspheming through mimicking and mocking the Christ of God. The end of chapter 13 showed us that everyone would be forced to receive a mark for buying and selling; those who refused to worship the image of the first beast would be killed.

Introduction

In 14:1-20 there seems to be a response to much of the conflict in 13:1-18. John moves from a description of events that describe the incredible audacity of counterfeit truth—the ultimate evil—to a preview of the end of the story, so that those in the midst of the present evil age of persecution and suffering for Christ's sake, can hold on to the truth that the victory is sure and God is reigning.

Text

i) 14:1-5

(1) Before John provides assurance that God's victory will take place, he draws an immediate contrast between those who receive the mark of the beast and those who have the mark of the Lamb. The name on their foreheads is not that of the beast, but that of the Lamb and his Father. The importance of the mark lies in the assurance it gives believers; they will finally be victorious because of the blood of the Lamb. Unlike those who belong to the beast, they will be spared God's wrath. The contrast here implicitly points to the final destiny for the marked. This idea of destiny is more explicitly developed in verses 6 ff.

In verse 1 John sees the Lamb standing on Mount Zion with the 144,000 redeemed. Mount Zion is repeatedly referred to in the Old Testament as the place of deliverance; therefore, this vision is one of assurance. The number 144,000, as in chapter 7, probably symbolizes completeness. In other words, none who belong to God are lost through the persecution or death inflicted on them in chapter 13. This is not a select group of some spiritual favorites, but rather is symbolic of all of God's people, each having the Lamb's name written on his or her forehead.

(2-5) "And I heard a voice from heaven like the roar of many waters and like the sound of thunder." The sound John hears is probably that of the new song sung by the redeemed from the earth. It may be that God's people, the 144,000 redeemed from the earth, are the only ones privileged to learn the song. In these verses, we begin to run into a few questions concerning the identification of the 144,000. Is our previous interpretation of the 144,000 in chapter 7 as symbolic for all those with the name of the Lamb and his Father in jeopardy? Perhaps, these 144,000 are a distinct group from the wider context of God's people. If so, who would they be? Are they exclusively male and celibate?

It is perfectly justifiable to interpret "these are those who did not defile themselves with women" as symbolic. John is not intending elitism; he has the whole church in view. She has resisted the counterfeit attempts of the beasts to drive them to idolatry. It is this very intercourse of death that is depicted. These are believers who have not succumbed to the temptations of the pagan world to the point of defilement; they have followed the Lamb in contrast to following the world (a reminder here of several other New Testament passages which speak of the need to follow Christ in spite of counterfeiting tendencies in our midst). Those who are redeemed have been purchased and consecrated to God and to the Lamb through his blood. They are said to be blameless, having no lie found in their mouths. This is a preview filled with assurance and affirmation of God's love for each one who is his. Redemption and victory are real.

ii) 14:6-13

(6-7) John sees another angel flying over the earth, declaring an everlasting gospel. In this particular passage the good news of the end history and of God's grace should be at the forefront of our thoughts. Those who do not believe, as expressed by the now-familiar terminology of 'those who live on the earth,' are called to repent and worship God in the face of his imminent judgement. God is proclaimed in this context as both judge and creator, but the hour of his judgement is now upon them.

(8) In ushering in this judgement, a second angel now proclaims, "Babylon the Great is fallen...." Here, as in chapter 13, the connection should probably be made between Babylon and Rome. Just as the first beast is likely to represent Rome on one level, and yet on another level more than Rome, so here Babylon the Great represents an evil that has fallen from power. The wrath of God against the evil of the world cannot be averted forever and the day of judgment has now arrived.

(9-11) In proclaiming, "Fallen, fallen is Babylon the great..." the third angel clearly contrasts what is stated in 13:11-17. Previously, it was those who refuse to worship the image of the first beast that are to be killed. Now, however, justice is no longer delayed and those who refuse to worship the true God will face his wrath, a fate worse than death. Again, the Apocalypse highlights the importance of understanding that God's power is the greatest. It is from his wrath, not the destruction of the beast, that one must seek salvation; for those who persist in being enemies of God there will be torment with burning sulphur for a period of time in the presence of the Lamb and holy angels. The smoke of their torment lasts forever and there is no rest for those who worship the image of the beast or receive his mark. The angel's symbolic portrayal here is similar to that in Isa. 34:9-10 where Edom is destroyed as a result of God's judgement (Rev. 20:11-15).

(12-13) Obeying God and remaining faithful to Jesus are primary. Fidelity to the crucified and risen One and obedience to God (especially at this time of the Apocalypse) may result in horrendous persecution and even death. Yet the saints are repeatedly called to hold on to the assurance of God's ultimate power, authority, and salvation, and to remain steadfast in their devotion to God. "Blessed are the dead who die in the Lord from now on .... they will rest from their labor, for their deeds will follow them." This relates to verse 12 and bringing assurance to those who persevere.

Even if their faithfulness should bring them to their death in the midst of awful circumstances, this promise declares that they are fortunate. It is unlikely that 'from now on' infers a special status upon those who die during this period of time, as if all of God's people who have previously suffered from martyrdom are not fortunate. This beatitude furthers the truth that the Apocalypse brings blessing by repeatedly showing the faithful that their destiny is not in question. They are indeed fortunate.

The voice announcing, "from now on...." seems intent on assuring those facing martyrdom. If they do not worship the image of the beast they will be killed. However, this is not the end of the story. All who stand for Christ against the antichrist will, as the Spirit says, be given rest from the trials and sufferings brought upon them.

iii) 14:14–16

(14-16) Before rest comes, judgement must take place. The picture John uses here for judgement is one of a grain harvest, which I will say more about in the next section. First, it is important to recognize there is some debate concerning the identity of the one 'like a son of man' with the crown of gold and the sharp sickle. The fact that this one is commanded to carry out the reaping by another angel makes it unlikely that the one 'like a son of man' is the Christ. It is argued that Christ would not be ignorant that the time had come, nor has it been explained, if it is the Christ, why an angel would know more about God than Christ himself. Therefore, it is argued that the one 'like a son of man' is another angel, giving us seven angels in the chapter and keeping with John's symbolic use of sevens.

Others disagree, arguing the description 'son of man' sets this one apart from the other six angels in the chapter. In addition, 'son of man' is a phrase that is never applied to angels. This reference must be to the risen Christ. The angel comes out of the temple and should be viewed as God's messenger acting on his authority in delivering the divine decree that judgement is to begin. In relation to judgement we are told very simply "and the earth was harvested."

iv) 14:17-20

(17-20) In these verses two more angels arrive on the scene. The first comes out of the temple and has a sharp sickle. The second comes from the altar and has charge of the fire.

The second angel calls out to the first to take the sickle and harvest the grapes. Once this is done the grapes are thrown into the great winepress of God's wrath. They are trampled in the wine press outside the city, resulting in a massive amount of blood. The language and imagery here are related to judgement. The question is, whose judgement?

In order to respond to this question we need to review verses 14-16. Some argue that these verses speak of the general judgement of all humanity, that the reaping includes both the righteous and the unrighteous.

This view interprets these verses as referring to the end-time judgement carried out by the One 'like a son of man.' The term 'harvest' might be understood as it often is in the Old Testament and with the wheat and tares in the New.

The metaphor of harvesting can often refer in a more limited sense to the ingathering of the righteous into the Kingdom of God, while verse 17 shows how this judgement relates to the unrighteous using the same type of imagery in a more explicit way, confirming that all humanity is concerned.

Another view interprets verses 14-16 in this more restricted sense: the harvest is that of the righteous and only the righteous, but the wicked are punished in verses 17-20.

A final view depicts a more restricted meaning, but differs from the first and second views by arguing that verses 17-20 do not concern both the righteous and the wicked, but only the wicked.

Deciding which of these three exegetical options is the best concerning verses 14-16 and the harvest is an open question with no precise answer. Certainly, all three views agree the imagery in verses 17-20 deals with the judgement of the wicked.

To face the wrath of God will be to experience the end of all wrath. There is none greater, none more powerful and just. Remember, it is from this final wrath that those who are God's will ultimately be protected. There is no promise that in this world there will be a trouble free life, no promise that our present circumstances will be as they ought to be. In fact, we can expect to struggle and experience conflict, which is a clear sign that we are engaged in the battle.

Trusting God is never easy. We face the reality of spiritual battles, wilderness wanderings, the silence or sense of God's absence that sometimes permeates our lives. These conflicts tend to overwhelm us and disorient our path toward God. There may be a feeling that we are entirely on our own.

What is called for is patient endurance—the reorientation of holding on in the midst of what may be devastating, painful situations and resisting the subtle, but powerful urges and temptations to succumb to the evil that surrounds us. Despite what we are going through God is faithful.

As God's loved and subversive people, we need strength, patience, and wisdom to be able to live in trust and hope.

Summary of the *three* chapters:

Chapter 12

Upon Satan God inflicts a partial defeat. We discussed three different options in interpreting the chapter: the "S", "SL", and "SLE" views.

We concluded with *three* points. First, Exodus typology is used frequently in verses 4, 6, 14, 15, 16 and there is an allusion to Genesis 3:15 in verse 17. This being the case, the emphasis as all three interpretative possibilities pointed out, is God's faithfulness to his people shown throughout history.

Second, I offered the perspective that this chapter is concerned with expressing reality, the way things are, for God's people. Like the rest of the book, chapter 12 is not primarily concerned with the future in any exclusive sense; it is better to understand the past, present, and future as woven together. John is affirming what God is doing in the present and how eventually the complexities of the spiritual-earthly battle that constantly rages will be worked out: God has been, is, and will be victorious. Satan has been, is, and will be defeated.

Third, God's consummated rule is coming soon; it has not yet arrived. Evil persists. Satan roves around like a lion seeking to destroy those he can, but thanks be to God Satan's time is short.

God has provided a way for his people to overcome through the blood of the Lamb. Don't forget the context we're in. God's reign has begun, and the future has broken into the present, first through the work of Christ and now through the work of the Spirit in our lives. We are to be living and experiencing the victory of the Lamb today as we await the consummated rule of God in the future.

Chapter 13

In chapter 13 the dragon blatantly counterfeits the truth of God in the parody of the beasts. The parallels between Christ and the beasts cannot be missed. Who is like the beast; who can make war against him? Even the resurrection is mimicked!

We then saw an emphasis in verses 5-7 that God is reigning. Remember, we are told the beast was given its power four times in these verses. The aim however, is not to address the problem of evil, but to assure believers of God's power. Any power the beast has is given by God.

All the inhabitants of the earth whose names are not written in the Lamb's book of life will worship the beast. During this trial the saints are called to patient endurance and faithfulness. Remember, we associated the first beast with the Roman Empire, but did not limit it to this symbolism. If we limited ourselves to that association only, we would miss the importance of the beast being presented as the antichrist and therefore greater than the Roman Empire. Indeed, the Roman Empire was a particular manifestation of the antichrist, but not its full manifestation.

Here are some examples. The first beast is clearly more political than the second. It seems the second beast strives to delude people not so much through political power, but primarily through religious persuasion and force. We envisioned the second beast as a likely representation of the imperial cult as a false prophet. This second beast also was given power to give breath to the image (Gk. *eikon*) of the first beast and to cause all who refuse to worship the speaking icon (*eikon*) to be killed. At the end of the chapter the socio-economic factor was brought in; it is necessary to have the beast's mark to buy and sell. We concluded that God's rule and mark are concerned with the political, social, and economic areas of life, not just the spiritual.

Chapter 14

There is an explicit contrast between those who are marked in chapter 13 and those marked in this chapter. The message is simple; regardless of the circumstances God will protect his people. Final destiny is ultimate. God's wrath is the wrath we need to fear, not that of the antichrist. Final judgement is coming. Are we ready for the fallout should it occur in our lives? We should be. Ultimate victory through the blood of the Lamb is ours to share. Praise God! He has revealed to his people the end of the story. Remember, the story ends with God's victory through the Lamb, a present reality to be lived in all areas of life now.

THE SEVEN ANGELS & THE LAST PLAGUES (15:1-8)

General Review

In chapters 12, 13, and 14 we came to the end of John's visions concerning the church and its struggle against evil. In the midst of this struggle we must not forget the ultimate battle is between God and Satan. The final outcome is that God and the Lamb are victorious, and believers are repeatedly assured of this victory throughout the Apocalypse. We who are Christians are called to base our lives upon this victory and to live it out in the present evil age.

Introduction

It is important to note that chapter 16 will help us understand chapter 15 more clearly as it seems to function as an introduction to the seven bowls of God's wrath. Similar to the trumpets of chapters 8 and 9, chapter 16 is couched in Exodus typology. Previously, we understood the effects of God's judgement on the world as partial. The judgement in chapter 16 now becomes more dramatic and the effect is total. The seven bowls of wrath are the last in the series of seven seals and seven trumpets that reveal God's judgement.

Corresponding to previous chapters, clear allusions to the Exodus are found in chapter 16: painful sores (Ex. 9:10); waters turning to blood to (Ex. 7:17-21); darkness (Ex. 10:21); frogs (Ex. 8:2); and finally a refusal to repent (Ex. 9:34). All this Old Testament language seems to indicate that the great events of God's judgement on Egypt were a foretaste of his mighty final judgement on the world.

Text

i) 15:1-8

(1) It is after the harvesting of the earth that we are introduced to another great sign. The seven angels with seven plagues may be attempting to signify the completion of God's wrath, the last in the series. The final image of seven brings to completion what the previous ones only prepared for.

(2) John saw what looked like a sea of glass. This time the sea is mixed with fire, which is difficult to understand. Some consider fire a reference to judgement while others maintain it is a heightening of the magnificence of John's vision.

Beside or on the surface of the sea are those who are said to have been victorious over the beast, his image, and the number of his name; they have held out and not succumbed to the beast's mighty power and authority. The victory, while not explicitly explained here, is accomplished by the blood of the Lamb, and those who are victorious are those who have a responsibility to resist and overcome evil.

(3) The victorious are given harps and sing the song of Moses and the song of the Lamb. It is a song of victory, a song of praise to God for his deeds and activity in the world. But are the songs of Moses and the Lamb two separate songs? It seems unlikely. Notice the clear parallels between the Exodus victory song in Exodus 15 and the songs here. This connection to Exodus notably corresponds to previous allusions of the plagues in reference to the outpouring of God's final wrath. God's judgement on Egypt was a foretaste of his wrath upon the inhabitants of the earth, just as the Exodus, the release of God's people from slavery, through the wilderness, and eventually into the Promised Land, was also a foretaste of God's redeeming purposes for his people. This liberation is ultimately fulfilled in the Lamb. John's intention may be to combine the great salvific acts of God, desiring to show the relationship between the foretaste and the fulfilment in this one song. Almost every phrase of the song has rich and meaningful Old Testament associations from the Psalms and prophets (Ps. 92:5, 111:2, 118:1, 134:4; Amos 4:13; Jer. 10:7).

(4) A rhetorical question is posed at the beginning of this verse. The expected answer is that all will fear and glorify God for he alone is holy. In reference to the next part of this verse, "All nations will come and worship before you," some would argue that it would be out of place to take this 'all nations' portion literally, as that would point toward universalism, a position not in keeping with the Apocalypse and the whole of Scripture. The argument is that this is a metaphor expressing God's greatness and victory over all enemies.

On the other end of the spectrum, others maintain that, "All nations will come and worship before you," is meant to be taken literally as it looks forward to the willing submission of all nations to God.

Another literal option is that the reference is not to a willing submission, but an unwilling one. All nations will be forced to bow before

God and to acknowledge that his righteous acts have indeed been revealed.

(5-6) John sees the temple in heaven revealed as the tabernacle of Testimony, which may connect to the post-Exodus presence of God being with his people in the giving of the Ten Commandments that were placed in the tabernacle, but this image now serves as ushering in judgement.

The angels, proceeding directly from the presence of God, are described as wearing royal-priestly garments, probably another sign that the judgements they are about to execute are to be carried out for the sovereign and ultimate purposes of God.

(7) One of the four living creatures gives to the seven angels seven bowls of the wrath of God. It is important to note that the word used here for bowl is the same word used in 5:8 where the bowl contains the prayers of the saints.

John may be, as in chapter 8, making the connection between the outpouring of the wrath of God and the prayers of the saints. If this is the case, the God who lives forever and ever interprets these prayers in executing his judgement on evil in all its forms.

(8) The verse is not so much a conclusion as it is an introduction to the end. The final outpouring of the wrath of God on the earth begins. His glory and power fills the temple with smoke indicating God's awesome power to carry out his just judgements.

No one is allowed to enter the temple as it is completely filled with the magnificence of God during this final and solemn outpouring of his wrath. The finality is striking and one can only conclude that the God of grace is also the God of justice. This will be made clear in chapter 16.

THE SEVEN BOWLS (16:1-20)

General Review

Chapter 15 is an introduction to the seven bowls that chapter 16 is going to present in detail. Again, the seven bowls of wrath are the last in a series of sevens in this book, including the seals in chapter 6 and the trumpets in chapter 8. Both chapters lead up to the finality of God's wrath poured out in chapter 16 and the chapters following.

Introduction

Let me remind you again of the clear allusions John uses in Revelation to the Exodus: painful sores (Ex. 9:10); waters turning to blood (Ex. 7:17-21); darkness (Ex. 10:21); frogs (Ex. 8:2); and the refusal to repent (Ex. 9:34). In my opinion, the ubiquitous use of Old Testament language purposes to demonstrate how the great events of God's judgment on Egypt were a foretaste of his final judgment on the whole world.

Of course we must remember, as chapter 15 makes amply clear, the Exodus was not merely judgment on Pharaoh and Egypt, but also resulted in the dramatic liberation of God's people who were brought out of Egypt and eventually, after a period of wilderness wanderings, into the Promised Land flowing with milk and honey. With this an important backdrop for understanding, let us look more closely at the text of this chapter.

Text

i) 16:1-9

(1-2) The seven angels are commanded to "go and pour out the seven bowls of God's wrath on the earth." The action begins without hesitation. The first angel's bowl is poured out on the land afflicting people with painful and ugly sores.

Notice those afflicted are those who bear the mark of the beast and worship his image, demonstrating a selectivity regarding this plague. In my opinion, because of this noted distinction of those with the mark, John is giving fairly clear exegetical evidence that believers are still on the earth at this time.

(3-4) The second angel pours out his bowl into the sea and all living things in the sea die. In contrast to 8:9 when a third of the creatures in the sea were destroyed, now 'all' living creatures of the sea die, affirming that these plagues are final.

The third angel's bowl, similar to the third trumpet in 8:10, affects the fresh water. Again, this demonstrates the previous plague is intensified. This third bowl is similar to the third trumpet in 8:10. Previously, the water was merely made bitter, now it has turned to blood; previously only a third of fresh water was affected; now the effect is total.

(5-6) The angel in charge of the waters proclaims the righteousness of God's activity. This unusual reference to an angel in charge of natural elements is reminiscent of Jewish thought (1 and 2 Enoch). It occurs three times in the Apocalypse (once in 7:1 where angels hold back the winds, once in 14:8 concerning fire, and once here). The proclamation is very similar to the victor's song in 15:3-4 where righteousness, holiness, and the justice of God's ways and judgments are noted.

Notice again, as in 11:17, God is the One who is and was. The familiar future reference, 'who is to come' is now excluded. This affirms that the final outpouring of his wrath has arrived. The proclamation concludes by showing the outcome for those who have shed the blood of believers. Those who have shed the blood of the saints are forced to drink it.

(7) The altar is used here to signify and highlight the remarkable importance of the prayers of the saints in relationship to the ultimate judgment of God (6:9-10). The affirmative response concerns the previous proclamation: "Yes, true and just are the Lord's judgments."

(8-9) As with the fourth trumpet blown in 8:12, the fourth bowl concerns the sun. In God's final judgment the sun will scorch the people of the earth; the heat will be unbearable.

We should notice the passive verb 'was given' in reference to the power of the sun. What is taking place is not merely a cosmic occurrence of an unexplained nature, but the just judgment of God.

As Pharaoh refused to repent, to change his heart, and glorify God, so too those who are afflicted with these plagues refuse to repent. In the raging battle of sovereignties there is again clear reference to the fact that God is reigning.

Despite pollution and the depleting of the ozone, or some other environmental phenomenon, the world has not simply been spun into chaos. God is moving history to its end. God's final judgment has come upon human beings, and obstinately failing to recognize their sin, all they do is blaspheme and curse his name. Drama increases as we see what unfolds next.

ii) 16:10–16

(10-11) The fifth angel pours out God's wrath on the throne of the beast, shifting the focus of the plagues toward political catastrophe, whereas the previous plagues have been related to human beings and nature. The description of the kingdom of the beast being plunged into darkness may be a reference to Rome's political unrest and the doubts, terrors, and chaos which surrounded the empire at various times of turmoil and uncertainty. It is possible that again, as in chapter 13, some of the things relevant to John's own situation were a preview of the coming wrath and that there is a darkness of further intensity at the time of God's final wrath. It is important to remember that just as the previous plagues were not simply the result of human activity or ecological disasters, neither is the darkness merely the result of political turmoil, but is a direct judgment of God. Again, the result will be that God is blasphemed and there is a refusal to repent.

(12-13) As with the sixth trumpet blown in 9:14, the sixth bowl is poured into the great river Euphrates. In this context the river is dried up, not to prepare the way of salvation as often in the Old Testament, but to prepare the way for the enemy, portrayed here as "the kings of the East." These kings symbolize Israel's traditional enemies who threatened destruction of God's people.

We have previously connected the dragon, the beast, and the beast of the earth, or false prophet in chapters 12 and 13, with the imperial cult. It is probable there is a relationship here between the frog-like spirits proceeding from their mouths and the propaganda associated with the imperial cult and its emperor worship. The text also speaks beyond John's immediate world, for the dragon, the beast, the false prophet, and these evil spirits all have a part in the final battle between the forces of good and evil.

(14) These spirits use their power to perform signs, influencing the kings of the world to gather for battle on the great day of Almighty God. The *great* day is important; it signifies the *last* day. The term 'almighty' is also important. It is God, not humans, not the dragon, the beast, or the false prophet, who is supreme. The proclamation in 11:16-17 refers to this supremacy where the twenty-four elders worship God saying, "We give thanks to you, Lord God Almighty, the One who is and who was, because you have taken your great power and have begun to reign." The sixth bowl brings us to the great and terrible day of the Lord prophesied in the book of Joel. Who can endure it? Who can stand? In the midst of the wrath of God coming upon the world, the answer in the Apocalypse has been clear. Those who can stand, those who can endure are those who believe in the Lord Jesus Christ, the Lamb of God whose blood has been shed for the sins of the world. Their endurance is situated in the truth that they are sheltered from that which could finally destroy them.

(15-16) The words of Jesus, the Lamb of God, similar to those of 3:3 are interjected in the midst of the outpouring of God's wrath. A beatitude announces that those who stay awake with their clothes nearby are fortunate. We can take this to mean that believers are explicitly addressed, being cautioned against being caught unprepared (naked and sleeping) when Jesus comes. They must stay awake and be alert to Christ's coming and the final battle on the great day. These verses heighten the drama as they depict forces on both sides getting ready for the denouement.

John returns to his description of the enemy, the 'they' of verse 14.

'They' are the evil spirits who gather the kings together for the final battle in the place called Armageddon. There is much discussion about this name and place. We are left with a mystery and cannot be precise. The basic meaning of the word is mountain of Megiddo. Megiddo is a small town in Israel, but there is no mountain nearby. Mount Carmel is the closest, yet is ten kilometers away. However, there is no evidence that Carmel was ever referred to as Megiddo.

To be too geographically or literally-minded may be a misuse of John's use of symbolism. Whatever the origin of the word or wherever it takes place, the point is that this place called Armageddon will be the place of the final battle between the kings of the earth and Almighty God.

iii) 16:17-21

(17) The last bowl is poured into the air. There is much that is similar to the seventh trumpet in 11:15 ff, but again the effects of the last bowls are terminal, rather than partial. The voice out of the temple and from the throne proclaims, "It is done." The details of exactly what has been done and the specific consequences of this final bowl will be explained in chapters 17 and following. The general effect of this finality is outlined in verses 18-21.

(18-21) As experienced in the seals and trumpets previously, lightning, rumbling, peals of thunder, and an earthquake come after the seventh in the series of sevens: the seventh seal, the seventh trumpet, and now the seventh bowl. However, the scope of the earthquake has devastating universal effects. Everything collapses and the whole earth is in a pile of ruins. God's wrath has come and all is devastated. The great city, probably Rome, is split into three parts and the cities of all the nations collapse. God remembers the sins of Babylon the Great, and the city is given the cup of his wrath for he will not forget the treatment his people have received at the hands of evil. Coupled with the earthquake is a huge hailstorm, the extent of which causes human beings again to curse God.

To understand chapters 15 and 16 it is important to remember the Exodus typology used, reminding us of God's great salvific activity on behalf of his people. If God protected Israel during the plagues on Egypt, will he not continue to protect his people from the ultimate and final outpouring of his wrath at the end? His judgment is true and just. He is the Holy One who will avenge the spilt blood of his saints and his prophets. Fortunate are those who stay awake for the Christ will return when he is least expected. We who believe must stand firm to the end. Do not be deceived. God remembers his people and hears their cries. Hold fast to the victory which is his and, through the blood of the Lamb, ours to share!

THE WOMAN, WISDOM, & VICTORY FOR THE LAMB (17:1-18)

Introduction

Consider chapters 17 and 18 as a unit that corresponds to and expands on the fall of Babylon the Great. As in previous chapters, chapter 17 is full of highly symbolic language. This time there is a depiction of the judgment of the great harlot who sits on many waters. Let us try to decode this chapter with an emphasis on both the original context as well as its application for us.

Text

i) 17:1-6

(1) In continuing with the themes of chapter 16, it is one of the seven angels who speaks to John and shows him what the proceeding judgment entails. It is important to note that it is also one of the seven angels who

shows John the bride of the Lamb (21:9). On the basis of 17:15, it becomes clear that the many waters upon which the great harlot sits are really peoples, nations, multitudes, and languages, and we should keep this in mind as it will be important for the interpretation of the chapter.

The identification of the great harlot in the first century context is probably representative of Rome, robed in wickedness and self deification, a type of ancient Babylon in all its godlessness. The thrust of this book remember is eschatological, focusing on the future manifestation of the victory of God over evil. Both Babylon and Rome were great in their wickedness and their persecution of the people of God, but neither had the power to seduce the whole world to worship the beast and his image. That great seduction is still to come. We await the final manifestation of ultimate ungodliness. It will come subtly, but with great power and ubiquitous deceit.

(2) Because kings and kingdoms represent political, social, and economic power structures and ideologies, the association of the great harlot with the 'kings of the earth' reveals the adulterous association of all aspects of life with the attitudes and convictions of the great harlot, Babylon, Rome, and beyond.

In the second part of verse 2 John returns to the phrase 'the inhabitants of the earth,' a constant reference in this book to those who reject God and his Christ. They are drunk on the adulterous relationship; they have allowed themselves to become enticed and seduced by the wine of madness, destruction, and death (Jer. 51:7). They are one with the great harlot in her ungodliness.

(3a) After the description of the harlot, John is actively carried away in the Spirit by the angel. 'In the Spirit,' a phrase we have already seen in this book, is describing a paranormal state not simply related to being a Christian. John is making a point that something extraordinarily unique is taking place when his visions come 'in the Spirit.'

(3b-6) John is 'in the Spirit' when he gives a further description of the woman: the harlot is sitting on a scarlet beast, probably the same beast as in 13:1 (the second beast). The color scarlet may correspond to the color of the dragon in 12:3, likening the relationship of the beast to the dragon. John wants his readers to clearly envision a chain of evil so that they realize these manifestations are not merely random, but rather a concerted and unified plot aiming to dethrone God and destroy his people.

The beast is full of blasphemous names, perhaps a reference to its self deification. It has seven heads and ten horns, similar to the dragon in chapter 12. The great harlot is arrayed in all the splendor of worldly possessions. She holds in her hands a golden cup full of detestable things.

As referenced previously in this book, John again mentions that a name is written on the forehead of the woman, recalling to mind how this phrase is used in reference to the followers of God (7:3) and the followers of the beast (13:17) revealing the ultimate allegiance of its bearer. This time the name is prefaced by "mystery" followed by "Babylon the Great, mother of prostitutes and of the abominations of the earth." Babylon the Great represents all that is ungodly and corrupt and is not merely content in its own evil, but repeatedly gives birth to more and more evil throughout the earth.

There is a relationship between the name of the woman to the saints. The saints are those who bore witness to Jesus. She is who she is because she is drunk with their blood.

In my opinion, this graphic reference speaks of widespread bloodletting based on primarily religious grounds, surpassing any evil that has taken place in regard to the persecution and martyrdom of the saints. Those final days will be appallingly awful. In the last part of the verse John's astonishment may be due to what he has seen in contrast to what he was expecting. The judgement of verse 1 has not yet begun and the description of evil manifesting itself up to this point is horrific.

ii) 17:7-18

(7) The angel responds to John's astonishment with an explanation of the identity of the woman and the beast she rides. Both the woman and the beast are linked closely together, for they are as one and should be understood as intimately related at this stage. The angel speaks of the beast first. The allegory and symbolism in verse 8 ff is explained with further symbolism.

(8) Twice in this verse the description, "once was, now is not and will come," serves as a jolting reminder of the parodies in chapter 13. The entire world, except those whose names are written in the book of life, will be astonished to see the beast. The beast rises up out of the Abyss, signifying his evil origins. This is no ordinary beast, but a satanic beast representing all that is evil and ungodly. It is important to note that the beast's ascension out of the Abyss is toward destruction showing that in the midst of satanic evil and oppression there is assurance of its defeat.

(9-10) As well as the importance of understanding that the beast faces imminent defeat, it is also necessary to have wisdom concerning the number of the beast and John's imagery to be able to remain faithful (13:18). The explanation of the imagery in verse 9 goes on to point out the seven heads are seven hills upon which the woman sits. It seems likely that most first century readers would have readily understood this depiction as Rome, the city built on seven hills. The imagery is stretched further; the seven hills are also seven kings: five have fallen, one still stands, and the other king has not arrived.

How are we to understand this description? Many think this image of seven hills is a reference to a list of Roman emperors. The fallen five could perhaps be Augustus, Tiberius, Caligula, Claudius, and Nero; the one who still stands is Vespasian, and Titus is representative as the one who has not yet arrived to reign. The problem with this scheme is that it requires leaving out three legitimate emperors between Nero and Vespasian, starting with Augustus, not Julius Caesar. Even if this list of possible rulers is accepted as references, there are irresolvable problems with dates as John did not write until later after these men had come to power.

Others would argue that the seven kings are not kings, but seven successive kingdoms including: Egypt, Nineveh, Babylon, Persia, and Greece as the five fallen; Rome, the kingdom that still stands; and kingdom to come will have a short reign and refers to all anti-God governments from Rome to the empire of the antichrist. The problem with this interpretation is that the word 'kings' is *basileus* not *basileia*, or 'kingdoms,' and we are left with the same kind of arbitrary choice as before when it comes to where the list should begin.

In the light of the problems posed by our previous considerations, it is perhaps best to see the seven kings as symbolic for completeness as are most of the other sevens in this book. The intention of the explanation is not to give a past tabulation of kings, but to demonstrate the close proximity of the end. A better symbolic interpretation may be that the seven kings stand for the entire epoch of Rome's tyrannical reign, of which the end is now near, and further for the total period of the despotic influence of ungodliness.

(11) The beast that once was, and now has been destroyed, is said to be an eighth king. As we have seen, it is unlikely that this is a reference to a specific emperor. The Emperor Domitian may be a possibility, but if this were the case he would only represent the beast within the limited capacity of his reign as he was likely to have been the emperor during the time John received these visions. Remember, that the beast 'now is not' is mentioned twice in 17:8 and once here.

In other words, the complete Antichrist has not yet come up out of the Abyss. All antichrists that have come before (Babylon, Rome, Antiochus Epiphanes, Nero, etc.) are only a part of the a more profound and threatening evil that will arise in the eighth king who was, now is not, and is yet to come. He is related to the seven kings in that he is their successor in world domination, but he is distinct from them in that he is the one who comes out of the Abyss.

This reminds us of 13:14-17 where the beast who appears is slain and therefore 'is not,' but is also yet to come to deceive and to force all to worship him or be killed. What appears to have been destroyed in the beast is not! The antichrist lives on for the final battle.

These verses in chapter 17 speak of the nearness of the end when the final manifestation of evil and ungodliness comes, its rule will be short. The beast 'is not' in the sense 'he was' at John's time, but this does not mean there will not to be other types of beasts that pre-figure the antichrist who comes out of the Abyss.

(12-13) The ten horns represent ten kings who have not yet received their power. When they do, it will be for a short time and they will be fully aligned with the beast (verse 13). Likewise, as with previous imagery, this picture of ten kings seems unlikely to be a timetable of Western European history.

The point of the ten kings is not that we should be looking at some allegiance of ten. The point is that we should realize all the world's powers will eventually be subject to and conformed to the beast. Believers want to be aware of this trajectory so that they are not lulled into a false sense of security.

(14) It now becomes clear that everything evil, spiritual, and material, makes war against the Lamb. However, the Lamb will overcome in this final battle of good and evil (look back to 16:16 and Armageddon). After all, he is Lord of lords and King of kings. His kingship and kingdom are more powerful than any evil in existence. His lordship is incomparable; it extends throughout the cosmos.

The Lamb's victory is not his alone. It is shared by those who are with him: the called, chosen, and faithful. The adjective 'faithful' should be important to us. Called and chosen are also important, but faithful, mentioned last, is of central importance in relationship to the whole of the Apocalypse where believers are exhorted over and over to hold on in the midst of grave circumstances. Victory is assured in spite of what may appear to be defeat.

(15-16) The angel continues with his explanation to John. The harlot who sits on the waters is sitting on peoples, nations, multitudes, and languages, suggesting her universal authority and impact.

Again, in John's context the harlot is probably the capital city Rome, while the beast is the ultimate manifestation of personal, political, social, and economic evil. However, remember both the capital city and the beast are types of evil looking forward to eschatological fulfilment. In each manifestation, the power of evil will be stronger and more horrendous as the end of history draws near and the ultimate eschatological battle takes place.

In an attempt to capture total power and authority the beast (Ezk. 23:25-30) who 'now is not' has come, and the beast and the ten horns surprisingly turn on the harlot, ultimately destroying her.

(17-18) There is a reminder that it is God who is reigning over the final historical battle. History is moving to his desired outcome. The world is not in utter chaos and disarray, and the reigning God's words will be entirely fulfilled.

The explanation culminates with the affirmation that the woman John has seen is the great city that rules over the kings of the earth. No doubt for John this city in his own day corresponds to Rome, but as we have seen previously in the Apocalypse, this imagery cannot be only limited to it.

In the last days eschatological Babylon and Rome will arise, but just as ancient Babylon and Rome fell, so too will this city. God will bring his righteous judgement upon this mighty manifestation of evil, devastating it, as his reign continues towards consummation and the renewal of all things.

There is much talk today about a one world government being put forward, but it is difficult to read all the logistics and organizational patterns that might allow for this to happen. The UN, for example, may be quickly becoming a vehicle for this kind of one world rule.

Furthermore, economic links between countries are already in place as global trading now occurs twenty-four hours a day and the proliferation of marketing increases the trajectory of a greater unification of the whole world.

However, we should not be too sure that all movement in this direction means the coming of the end. I've heard, for example, much about one political figure or another being the antichrist. This is not an impossibility, but we have to wait and see what the future holds.

We should neither be reading every event on the world's stage as end times prophecy, nor should we be naive. This calls for minds of wisdom and hearts of patient endurance, so that we can continue to trust in both God's faithful working out of his purposes and the victory that believers already participate in because of the blood of the Lamb.

BABYLON FALLS (18:1-24)

Introduction

Chapter 18 is meant to be read with chapter 17 as it describes the *judgement* of the great harlot that has been expected since 17:1. In chapter 18, not only is it what John sees that is important, but also what he hears. Much of the chapter has its background in the Old Testament (Ezk. 26-28 concerning the fall of Tyre and Isa. 13-14 concerning the fall of Babylon) and is expressed here in what is known as a prophetic dirge or doom song. A fair amount of detail in the song/dirge now makes explicitly clear what we have already been told in 17:16-17.

Text

i) 18:1-3

(1-2) Another mighty angel (also represented as a Christlike figure) who has great authority and splendor enters. The angel calls out in a mighty voice, "Fallen, fallen is Babylon the Great," reminiscent of 14:8

(Isa. 13:20, 21:9). Babylon, depicted as fallen (in the past tense), affirms a future fulfilment throughout the Apocalypse. Babylon *will* be sacked. God's purposes are so sure of accomplishment there is no reason to distrust him. The fall of Babylon has resulted in her becoming the dwelling place of demons and a place for much that is unclean. The angel's portrayal is intended to depict Babylon as the peak of evil. Her power, authority, and influence over others are to be clearly understood.

(3) Babylon is destroyed because her pervasive evil entices "all nations" to participate in this intercourse with death. The kings of the earth have been seduced into false worship of the beast and as a result the merchants of the earth have profited and worship money, not God.

ii) 18:4-8

(4) John hears another voice from heaven announcing with Old Testament portrayals of God's great acts of salvation and judgement, that which is about to take place (Isa. 48:20, 50:8). God's people are warned to come out of Babylon for two specific reasons expressed in two 'so that' clauses. They must separate themselves so that they do not share in the sins of the great city and so that they will not receive the plagues of devastation. This verse could be referring to a literal physical departure or to a spiritual disengagement.

In either case the warning remains: believers must refuse to compromise with the forces of evil, and with the things, people, and institutions which promote death. Think of the many issues in our own day that promote death including homosexuality, divorce, and prosperity theology. In regards to these issues, Christians and others seem to be gradually accepting the stance that modern society is the final authority and therefore determinative of our views. In many churches today, gay marriage is encouraged, astronomical divorce rates are accepted, and prosperity is peddled and idolized as a clear sign of worth and value. However, Christians are called (and are to call others) out of the disorder, out of the evil and sin of a world gone mad with self indulgence and idolatry.

(5-8) Believers are reminded of the fact that God will not forget the sins of Babylon, which are so great they are said to be piled up to heaven. The speaker calls for judgement when the voice says, "To give back to her" is "to give back what she deserves." Both Babylon in the Old Testament and Rome in the New were oppressive regimes known for their greed and treachery; both have shed the blood of prophets and saints as will the final manifestation of the evil city in the last days. Such evil deserves a full measure of punishment and judgement from God.

Babylon is saturated with pride and self importance. She is proud of her victories and her seeming indestructability. This is reminiscent of ancient Babylon's arrogance in Isaiah 47:7-8. As previously, the pompous and haughty nation will be dealt with severely. It is exactly *because* of these things that the plagues will bring destruction. The disaster will come suddenly and unexpectedly. Consummation is totally inevitable as the mighty Lord God brings about judgement.

iii) 18:9-19

(9-10) These verses include the post-Babylonian destruction and future-orientated three-fold lament of the kings of the earth, the merchants, the sea captains, and the sailors. The kings of the earth are those who have committed adultery with the harlot by participating in ungodly activities and open rebellion against God. They stand in awe that

Babylon's destruction could come so suddenly, weeping and mourning over the loss of their supposed luxury, wealth, and power. However, they will not come to her aid or sacrifice themselves for her sake, but stand far off crying "Woe! Woe!" (verse 16).

(11-17a) The merchants too will weep and mourn for their loss of revenue as their market completely collapses. Much has been written about the luxurious lifestyle of Rome and the extravagances of its banquets and parties. The Romans were wealthy enough to spend massive amounts of money and the staggering volume of goods bought provided merchants with much of their income.

It is worth mentioning a few things on this list of imports to have some idea of the purchasing power of Roman society in John's day. Gold, silver, fine linen, silk, etc. were status symbols to a Roman citizen. Many of these imports were from around the world. Africa, China, Egypt, Phoenicia and other locations all had great trade with Rome (Ezk. 27). Along with fine textiles and precious metals, human beings were considered to be merchandise as much as any other commodity. The slave trade may have been the most profitable and prized of all, and some estimates indicate there were massive numbers of slaves in the Roman Empire. It is important to note that the phenomenal amount and tremendous variety of imports made Rome the center of the world and gave the city a sense of greatness, arrogance, and power, leading it to believe that its reign would never come to an end.

As the kings of the earth call for intervention in verse 10, so too the merchants will not seek to help, but rather stand far off frozen with terror. They too will weep and mourn crying, "Woe! Woe!"

(17b-19) The song/dirge is picked up by all those involved in the shipping industry and all those who earn their living from the sea. They too will stand at a distance and weep and mourn crying, "Woe! Woe!"

These people provided Rome with access to its material wealth while in turn being richly rewarded for their efforts.

iv) 18:20-24

(20) Here, the rejoicing that comes next is a stark contrast with the previous laments. Rejoicing comes from the fact that justice is done. The city has been judged, especially for its treatment of the saints, prophets, and apostles. Forces of evil are now being systematically and entirely destroyed. The great city of Satan, the epitome of ungodliness portrayed as ancient Babylon or as present Rome in John's day, or even as the future world-wide reign of Antichrist will be fully and utterly destroyed. Rejoice! Indeed, rejoice! God's rule is manifesting itself as the final day of judgement draws ever closer.

(21-23) Symbolically, a mighty angel shows what the impending destruction is to be like. To throw a large stone in the sea is reminiscent of Jeremiah's command to Seraiah in reference to the sacking of ancient Babylon (Jer. 51:59). All Jeremiah had written concerning the coming devastation of Babylon was to be read, have a stone tied to it, and be thrown into the Euphrates. As certainly as the stone sank, so too would Babylon's entire existence be removed from the earth.

The city's desolation is emphasized by its utter silence and non-activity. Lamps will no longer give light and marriage becomes non-existent. The six 'will never' statements in these verses ring out with an eerie finality. Life in Babylon will cease to exist. Judgement has come and death lurks over the once great city that boasted it would never mourn.

(24) This verse affirms that the blood of the prophets and saints has been spilled. As Babylon exercises worldly reign, metaphorically she becomes responsible not only for the death of prophets and saints, but

for all who have been killed. The centralizing of the blood of all the dead reinforces the picture of this city as a persecutor of those who would not adhere to its evil ways.

In chapter 18 God is judge, this fact and its results give the saints cause to rejoice. To the glory of God, the persecutor has become the judged. God will not leave evil alone, but will bring judgement and eventually vindicate his people, consequently affirming his glory.

HALLELUJAH & THE RIDER ON THE WHITE HORSE (19:1-21)

General Review

In some sense, the Fall of Babylon still awaits completion. Chapter 17 described the woman and the beast on which she was riding in somewhat coded language. It was pointed out in 17:14 that the ten kings and the beast will make war against the Lamb, but the Lamb will be victorious. Then the beast and the ten kings will turn against the great harlot and destroy her, a result of God putting his purposes in their hearts in order to fulfil his words (17:15-16).

The genre of chapter 18 is a prophetic dirge or doom song. It speaks of Babylon's fall as an already-completed act, but also insinuates that it is an event to come. This is consistent with apocalyptic literature in announcing the event as accomplished, even though its completion has not yet occurred. In verse 4 God's people are warned to leave Babylon so that they will not share in either her sins or the plagues which are coming. Babylon will suffer for her evil: the suddenness of her devastation will be mind-boggling.

The kings, the merchants of the earth, and all who earn their living from the sea will weep and mourn as these adulterous relationships come to a devastating end. As a result, Babylon has been justly judged and the saints, prophets, and apostles are called to rejoice. A picture of this resolution culminates as a mighty angel throws a large millstone into the sea in a symbolic act representing the violence, silence, and the ultimate death of the great city of Babylon.

Introduction

Chapter 19 is directly related to the two previous chapters. At this point in the Apocalypse we should strive more than ever to have a heightened awareness of the connections between chapters. Noticing these links will help bring the drama of what God has done into clearer perspective. The first five verses of chapter 19 are a good example.

Text

i) 19:1-5

The rejoicing in heaven by the great multitude corresponds directly to 18:20. It stands, as we said earlier, in marked contrast to the previous song/dirge of the kings, merchants, and seamen.

(1-2) It is again necessary to focus on what John hears, not only what he sees. We are not told who the multitude is; John only writes that he hears what sounded like the roar of a great multitude in heaven. This sound is reminiscent of what John has heard back in 14:2 where the multitude is the 144,000. The roar of the great multitude is clearly significant. In the entire New Testament, 'Hallelujah' is only mentioned here and again in verses 3, 4, 6. It means 'praise God!' In this context, salvation, glory, and power belong to him for two reasons expressed by two 'for' clauses.

First, God is to be praised, "for his judgements are true and just." His consummated kingdom is one step closer to realization. In conjunction with this consummated kingdom comes judgement.

Second, 'for' (not in NIV) he has judged the great prostitute on the grounds that she has corrupted the earth by her adulteries and that she has shed the blood of God's servants. The great prostitute has received what she deserves.

We who are Christians must remember we too will be judged, but the difference is that we will not receive what we deserve. We are in many ways like the great harlot, having participated in and led others to indulge in various forms of idolatry and ungodliness. We deserve death and the wrath of God. However, because of the blood of the Lamb, we who believe have been freed from the penalty that we all deserve because of our rebellion and rejection of God. Yes, judgement is a reality, but so is the power and quality of the blood of the Lamb. Those of us who are in Christ are sheltered from the coming mighty wrath of God in both its present and future manifestations.

(3-4) Another 'Hallelujah!' is proclaimed, praising God that the city has been totally destroyed and left desolate. In response to this great act of judgment, the twenty-four elders and four living creatures fall down worshiping God, pronouncing "Amen" in agreement with what has come.

Hallelujah! Praise God (7:12).

(5) A voice comes from the throne, possibly belonging to one of the elders or the four living creatures saying, "Praise our God ..... ." The chorus in heaven is now to comprise everyone, as praising God extends to each person in his presence.

ii) 19:6-10

(6) John hears again what sounds like a great multitude. He now gives us a little more information about the sound (14:2), but again we are not told who the multitude is.

The fourth and final 'Hallelujah!' is shouted. This time the reasons seem to be broader than just the fall of Babylon. With the fall of Babylon the end-time reign of the Lord God Almighty has moved directly and devastatingly towards consummation. Remember though "God reigns" is likely to be a proleptic statement (similar to what we have seen previously concerning the fall of Babylon 14:8); it speaks of a future event as if it has already happened. A future event is also announced here. God reigns now in a limited sense as evil is yet to be totally destroyed. The broader perspective for praising God is that his reign will be complete as the end of the end draws closer to its goal.

(7) The nearing completion for God's kingdom calls for rejoicing and glorifying God, for the wedding of the Lamb has come and his bride has made herself ready. Again, this is proleptic; there is no description of the event, only the announcement that its time has come. The bride, that is all God's people, and the Lamb are betrothed to one another. They now await the consummation of the marriage as there is still more to be done before all is prepared and ready.

(8-10) Bright and clean fine linen contrasts with the purple and scarlet attire of the great prostitute. This pure linen 'was given' to the bride to wear. The last part of the verse may speak of the steadfast endurance of God's people. The bride of Christ makes herself ready through repentance, faithfulness, and righteous acts. Her righteousness is not to be solely attributed to herself because it 'was given' to her.

John is now commanded to write the fourth beatitude of the book; three more will follow. Those who are invited to the wedding supper of the Lamb are indeed fortunate because this messianic seal is a sign of the fulfilment of being with God forever. The angel adds, "These are the true words of God," possibly referring to all of what John has heard and seen from 17:1 including the climax here. John falls to worship the angel, but is strongly warned not to as the angel is just a fellow servant.

We too must consider what we are worshiping other than God, the created rather than the Creator. Life is so busy and there can be so much to worry about. How can we find any room left to worship God, praise him, and give him the glory?

Warning passages in the Apocalypse and the entire New Testament intend to capture our attention and transform our actions. The believing community is called to be aware and to put that awareness into practice.

John may understand "for the testimony of Jesus is the spirit of prophecy" to be connected to what he has been commissioned to write in the Apocalypse concerning who God was, is, and forever will be.

iii) 19:11-16

Heaven is opened and John sees a white horse whose rider is called Faithful and True. The rider on the white horse rides into the final victory, bringing the complete establishment of the *ultimate empire*.

(11-12) In righteousness he judges and makes war. With eyes like blazing fire, he sees all; nothing will escape his judgement. He is a King with many crowns, displaying his universal authority and power to make war against evil. He has a name known only to himself, for the fullness of the mystery of Christ no one can comprehend or completely understand. Although he can be known through revelation, who he fully is transcends our knowledge and remains something of an enigma.

(13-14) The rider on the white horse wears a robe dipped in blood (Isa. 63:1-6), probably the blood of his enemies. His name is the Word of God, the name through which and by which the Messiah was known. It is he who would be the revealed One, first in the incarnation in the gospel of John and now in the second coming. The armies of heaven follow him on white horses and are attired in a similar fashion as the righteous of verse 8.

(15-16) It is the Messiah alone who engages in the battle. "He strikes down the nations with a sharp sword" (Isa.11:4). This is not merely a battle of political and religious ideologies, but the inbreaking reign of God through which his consummated Kingdom will be established.

The promise that "He will rule them with an iron scepter" (Isa. 63:1 ff) affirms his awesome authority. "He treads the winepress of the fury of the wrath of God" (Isa. 63; Joel 3:13 ff) is another image of destruction. The name on his robe and thigh is crucial to his identity. "King of Kings, Lord of Lords" powerfully displays his universal power and dignity.

iv) 19:17-21

(17-19) God's universal provision is shown when the angel cries out to the birds to gather together for a feast, which God will provide through his coming victory (Ezk. 37:14-20). No doubt the language used provides a stark contrast to the wedding supper of the Lamb. The day of the Lord, compared with the image of the wedding supper, is horrific as his wrath is exceedingly great. The mighty battle is ready and the age-old war between good and evil is now to take place, the final step towards ultimate resolution.

(20-21) The battle, as such, never happens. The beast and false prophet are captured and thrown alive into the lake of fire. The armies of the beast and the kings of the earth are put to death by the sword of the rider. The terrible description includes birds gorging themselves on their flesh.

This chapter and its graphic depictions of justice may shock some of our pre-conceived notions about the 'King of Kings and Lord of Lords. It may challenge our concept of the Messiah and Jesus. Didn't Jesus come to love and forgive everyone?

With these questions in mind let us briefly consider again verses 11-16. In this section our perception of the Messiah is that he justly judges and makes war on his enemies. He is dressed in a blood-soaked robe and out of his mouth protrudes a sharp sword. He will rule nations with an iron scepter and he treads the winepress of the fury of the wrath of Almighty God. This is highly violent imagery, not to speak of the horrific scenes of 17-21. The enemies of Christ will not relent and must be overpowered. Christ's second coming will therefore be violent, resulting in much bloodshed and sudden death for those who have not taken refuge in the Lamb's own blood, as God's people had at the Passover in the Exodus.

We need to remind ourselves that God's work is not only about us as individuals, but relates to the wider world. God's work encompasses past, present and future, not just our individual experiences. He will do away with evil and all its representations to make everything new.

There is now only one more step; Satan himself will fall. Then God will fully dwell with human beings, for the old order of things that is now passing will have completely passed away. That is, the making of everything new has already begun in history through the cross of Christ and his glorious resurrection. In the future, as well as our present, God is fulfilling his plans to bring history to a close, bringing judgement and mercy to its consummated finality.

We who are Christians need not look to the consummation of God's rule in fear and trepidation. We too can shout, "Hallelujah!" for our Lord God Almighty reigns. Let us rejoice and be glad and give him the glory.

A THOUSAND YEARS (20:1-15)

Introduction

Chapter 20 is one of the most controversial chapters in the Apocalypse, or the whole Bible for that matter. There has been much ink spilt debating the meaning of the first six verses.

Before we delve into the text I want to provide a brief overview of some of the different ways in which these verses have been interpreted in correspondence with particular perspectives of the millennium, which refer to Christ's reign of a thousand years.

1) Premillennial: Dispensationalism

The first interpretation, dispensationalism, expects Christ to reign on the earth for a thousand years *after* he returns. The dispensational view centers around two factors:

i) a literal interpretation of prophecy.
ii) a distinction between Israel and the church.

In reference to Israel and the church it is clear that God has both earthly objectives related to Jews, and heavenly objectives related to the church. This view works out something like this: God's work and revelation falls into seven dispensations including innocence, conscience, human covenant, promise, law, the church, and the Kingdom.

Many of the promises in the Old Testament, dispensationalism argues, are specifically related to Israel, and are not to be understood as referring the church. There is the new covenant in Jeremiah 31:31-34 and other passages (Isa. 2:1-4, 11), which are said to point to a literal return of Israel to the land of Canaan at some point during the millennium during which time Jews will be blessed and live in peace under the earthly reign of Christ. At this time the temple will be rebuilt and animal sacrifices reinstituted as memorial offerings (Isa. 44:28). According to this view the church is an interlude between Christ's first coming and the rapture, and it exists because of the Jews' rejection of the kingdom of God as Christ preached it when he was on earth.

Dispensationalists usually look for Christ's second coming in two stages.

The first stage is the rapture, which can take place at any moment prior to the tribulation when God's judgment on his enemies begins (Cf. 4:1). Christians on the earth will be taken out and not live through the tribulation that is about to arrive. Christ is said to come only part of the way to earth at this time in order to call God's church to come up to heaven. According to dispensationalism this is when the resurrection of the believers who died and the transformation of all believers who are alive will occur.

In the second stage of Christ's second coming, the full return will take place only when Christ comes all the way down to earth in order to found and establish his millennial kingdom.

Here are the three major points of the dispensational view of this chapter:

a) There is a pre-tribulation rapture of Christians.
b) The coming of Christ is a two-stage coming—the first will be partial, the second complete.
c) God has different objectives for Israel and the church.

2) Postmillennialism: After the millennium

The second view, the postmillennial position, agrees with the next view, the amillennial perspective, that the millennium is not a literal thousand years. These two views also take the same stance regarding Christ's reign and coming; it is not an earthly one, and his return will be after the millennium.

Postmillennialists, however, differ in some major ways from amillennialists as we will see. The postmillennialist view understands the present age eventually becoming more and more Christian. The millennium will be expressed through a Christendom unlike the world has ever seen, where peace and righteous living culminate in the return of Christ.

This period of prosperity and harmony will go on for an undetermined time. Evil and sin will still exist, but the manifestations of them will be relatively minor until Satan is loosed at the end of this period, but even then the increase and manifestation of sin and evil will be rather trivial and the church will remain protected and unharmed.

There are three major points of postmillennialism:

a) Christ's reign is not an earthly one; the thousand years is not a literal thousand years.
b) The present age gradually becomes the millennium through the Christianization of the world, a period of time of peace and righteousness that will be followed by Christ's return.
c) Evil and sin will have a final manifestation but will be of little consequence.

While there are many interpreters who prefer to hold to dispensationalism or postmillennialism, neither view, in my opinion, is likely to best decode these complex verses. Therefore, we will not consider either of these interpretive options when we further explore this chapter.

3) Amillennialism: Realized millennialism

The third view, amillennialism, interprets the millennium as both future and present. Those who reign with Christ do so in heaven, not on the earth. This interpretation does not hold to a literal thousand-year reign of Christ on the earth and pictures the millennium as a figurative and symbolic period of time between the incarnation of Christ and the return of Christ.

An amillennialist believes that Christians will be on the earth during the tribulation period (they will not be raptured before this point in time) and that the second coming of Christ will be a single event, not occurring in two phases.

There are three major points of amillennialism:

a) The thousand years is figurative, representing the heavenly reign of Christ with raised believers.
b) The church is to live through the tribulation period and the subsequent persecution.
c) The second coming of Christ occurs as a single event.

4) Premillennialism: Historic

This perspective is identified as 'historic' because it argues that it has its roots in the early church and is therefore distinguished from the more recent (eighteenth century) expression, premillennialist dispensationalism. Furthermore, while both these views are premillennial they have clear differences including the place of Israel and the church.

According to historic premillennialism, there is no distinction between Israel and the church. Christ's return will be prior to the millennium and will take place in one stage, as opposed to two. After his return Christ will reign on the earth for a thousand years before the end comes. Historic premillennialists may differ from each other on a number of details, but most hold that before Christ's return there will be a period of tribulation in which the earthly church will experience persecution and oppression.

The church is to go through this period of oppression (others who are historic premillennialists believe that Christians are raptured and do not go through the tribulation), but when Christ comes all believers, Jews and Gentiles, living and dead, will reign with him on the earth for a thousand years.

During the millennial period sin and evil will still exist. However, both will be restrained by Christ so that this time will be marked by peace, justice, and prosperity as never before seen in the history of the world.

Near the end of the thousand years Satan will be loosed for the final battle. After the battle, unbelievers will be raised and face final judgement along with believers.

There are three major points of historic premillennialism:

a) The second coming of Christ is a one time event, and doesn't happen in two phases.
b) There is no distinction between Israel and the church; God has one people.
c) Christ will return before the millennium, but after the tribulation which the church must go through (some however, believe the church will be raptured before the tribulation).

Before getting into a more detailed exegesis of the chapter it is worth mentioning that there was much discussion amongst the ancient rabbis as to the possibility of a messianic reign prior to the end. In good rabbinic fashion, these debates included questions about the duration of such a reign and if it would arise out of history or come from outside it.

I mention this to emphasize the fact that these questions have been discussed throughout history and continue to be discussed today. We should not be too dogmatic about our interpretive ideas concerning these passages having the final word as to how they are to be understood.

Text

i) 20:1-3

(1) John sees an angel coming down from heaven with the key to the Abyss and holding a great chain. There is no great struggle here as Christ is not involved at this point, simply an unnamed angel on a mission.

(2) The angel seizes the dragon, who is the devil, and binds him for a thousand years. What does this mean? Some argue this is symbolic language describing a radical curbing of Satan's power for a period of time. Others understand it as Satan's complete inactivity for a thousand years after Christ's second coming.

(3) The first part of this verse, capturing Satan and locking him into the Abyss, may seem to affirm the view that Satan will now be inactive for a thousand years, until we come to the last part of the verse where we find that these previous acts were done to keep Satan from deceiving the nations. Could this mean that Satan was prevented momentarily and specifically from gathering the nations for the final battle?

Another possible interpretation is that the binding of Satan has already taken place in the first coming of Christ. This picture in 20:1 of the angel and the key is symbolic for Christ's mission on earth. While we may agree that Satan is bound to some degree with Christ's first coming, it seems unlikely that verse 1 is pointing us back to that.

More questions surface in attempting to decode the meaning of the thousand years. Do we take this time period literally or is it symbolic? A literal view interprets the thousand years as an exact reference to the time Christ will reign on the earth. The thousand year reign takes place after his second coming (premillennialism). If, however, this is symbolic, it may be referring to a period of time other than a literal thousand years between

Christ's first coming and his second coming (amillennialism). At any rate, Satan will be bound completely or partially for a period of time, unable to deceive the nations. After that time is finished, at God's choosing Satan is to be released for a short time.

My own perspective of the thousand years is the following: it seems to me we can hardly deny the fact that Satan is in some sense bound by Jesus' first coming (amillennialism). The power of Jesus was capable of binding the strongman, casting out demons, healing the sick, raising the dead, and forgiving sins (Isa. 61:1; Mt. 12:25, 22:4; Lk. 4:17). Jesus brought the rule of God with him by invading Satan's territory and showing us something of what God's rule was and will be. However, we must also affirm that Satan is active, prowling around like a lion seeking someone to destroy (1 Peter 5:8). Remember, in this book Satan is always bound to some degree by the fact that God is God and it is God who is reigning. Any power Satan has 'was given' and never possessed.

The point here is a theological one. Satan is bound in the general sense because God reigns. He is also bound, more specifically, by Christ's first coming. In addition to this, we read that he is to be bound here even more specifically from deceiving the nations.

The thousand years then need not be taken literally because numbers in the Apocalypse are often symbolic. For example, a thousand was a number used for completeness, which may simply be reinforcing the idea that Satan is bound from deceiving the nations and that God reigns over the final battle for a real period of time which he has determined. However, the symbolic sign of the number 1,000 need not necessarily negate the possibility that Christ will reign on the earth for literally a thousand years when he returns. Either way the emphasis is that God is reigning, and Satan is not.

ii) 20:4-6

These verses are complex and present us with a number of questions. How many groups does John see? Are those seated and those beheaded two separate groups? Some argue they are one and the same group. Since those mentioned in 13:15 who would not worship the image of the beast were killed, we have here an affirmation that the faithful will be seated on thrones and judge. It is they who have come to life and will reign with Christ for a thousand years.

Others argue for two groups: those seated are either the saints (1 Cor. 5:2-3), apostles (Mt. 14:28), or the heavenly court (Dan. 7:76). The second group is the martyrs. This possibility seems more likely. If this is the case, those seated on the thrones are believers who have died (3:21), while those beheaded are martyrs who would not necessarily be excluded from sitting on thrones. They receive special mention here in John's context (and also in all present and future contexts concerning the persecuted for the sake of Christ). This passage seems to emphasize that martyrs are not forgotten by God! The promise that they too will 'come to life' and reign with Christ seems a specific assurance to those facing horrendous persecution and ties in with the letters in chapters 2-3 regarding the need to overcome, even in the face of death.

(4) For the historic *premillennialist* position, the phrase "they came to life" means both the bodily resurrection of all believers and a literal thousand year reign on earth with Christ who comes back before the millennium. For the *amillennial* position it means a spiritual resurrection of all believers for a period of time between Christ's first and second comings. Christ's return will bring this period to a close.

(5) The parenthetical statement, "The rest of the dead did not come to life until the thousand year period of time was ended," is followed by,

"this is the first resurrection." Most commentators understand "the rest of the dead" to be the non-believing dead. The question is, when will these non-believing dead be raised? The *premillennial* position posits the dead will be raised after the literal thousand-year reign of Christ with the saints on earth, after the second coming. For the *amillennialist*, the non-believing dead will be raised; following the period of time between the first and second coming of Christ. That is, *at* Christ's second coming, rather than *after* it.

The next phrase, "this is the first resurrection" is usually thought of as referencing verse 4 concerning believers, especially martyrs. The question here is what kind of resurrection will this be? Will it be bodily, or spiritual, or will believers be regenerated on the earth? The language certainly has to be strained for the last possibility to be valid. As to whether nor not the resurrection will be bodily or spiritual, the language is unclear, making it difficult to decide.

As previously seen the words, "came to life" in verse 4 as well as "come to life" in verse 5 are at the center of the interpretive controversy. Our understanding of these phrases is crucial, but how is the *resurrection* to be understood?

To clarify, the *premillennial* position believes in a bodily resurrection of believers and a literal thousand- year reign with Christ on earth. The "rest of the dead," non-believers, are not raised until after the millennium in verses 11-13.

The *amillennialist* position disagrees, suggesting this phrase refers to the spiritual resurrection of believers who are to reign with Christ in heaven for a period of time between his first and second coming. The non-believers, or the "rest of the dead," will not be raised until the general resurrection that takes place in verses 11-13 at which time all people, believers, and non-believers will then be physically resurrected and subsequently judged.

(6) This verse affirms that those who take part in the first resurrection are fortunate and holy. The second death has no power over them. They are assured of being priests of God and of his Christ and will reign with him (1:4-8).

This is a wonderful and majestic picture of God's commitment to preserve life from everlasting to everlasting. There will be no limit to the access to God, and the life he offers will endure forever. His promises for those who follow in the footsteps of the crucified and risen One are going to be realized.

iii) 20:7-10

(7-10) At the end of the millennium, be it literal or symbolic, Satan will be released, no longer prevented from deceiving the nations. The end of the end is now at hand. Gog and Magog are biblical names for people or nations who rebel against God and are hostile to his people. Great numbers of these rebels surround the camp of God's people, in the city he loves.

The phrases "camp of the saints" and "beloved city" seem to symbolize God's people and they are probably not speaking of a literal camp or city, although many interpreters understand this as a reference to Jerusalem. The massive multitude of God's enemies has gathered, but no battle actually takes place. Fire comes down out of heaven and destroys those who oppose God and persecute his people. The devil, the great deceiver, is thrown into the lake of burning sulphur, joining the beast and the false prophet. Here, they will be tormented forever and ever. Satan is finally destroyed! Evil is cut off at its root; it can never grow again.

There is great assurance in these verses not only in John's context, but also in our own. God is the final victor and justice will be done. These pictures of ultimate victory are shockingly wonderful. God has provided us with a Lamb, his own son, whose blood was shed for both injustice and sin so that God might destroy his enemies and redeem his children.

iv) 20:11-15

(11) It is after Satan is finally destroyed that John sees a majestical scene of the great white throne and he who is seated on it. So great is his majesty that earth and sky are have fled because there was no place for them. The imagery is striking and intends to point out the awesomeness of God's final judgement.

(12-14) Premillennialists believe the judgement of these verses applies to "the rest of the dead." This view holds that non-believers are now bodily resurrected for final judgement. The *amillennialist* interpretation, however, posits this as a general bodily resurrection of believers and non-believers for final judgement. The dead, regardless of who they are, great or small, are before the throne, books are opened, including the book of life, and all are judged according to what they have done. Verse 13 re-emphasizes the scope of judgement, and verse 14 the finality of it. Death and Hades are thrown into the lake of fire, and experience the second death.

(15) The book of life is the key factor in this context of judgement, and throughout the Apocalypse. Remember, it is the Lamb's book of life and one can only be found in it because of the grace of God manifested through the blood of the Lamb.

THE NEW HEAVENS & NEW EARTH (21:1 - 22:21)

It is crucial to keep the prologue (1:1-20) in mind when studying these last chapters. There are many significant parallels that should not be missed. In chapter 20:11-15 the dead, including both believers and non-believers, are judged.

Those whose names were not found written in the book of life are thrown into the lake of fire and experience the second death. Satan suffers the same fate in 20:7-10 by joining the beast and the false prophet in their torment after the final battle. This torment is everlasting and is the final defeat and destruction of evil. In the war of sovereignties that has been being waged throughout this book, victory is now fully and ultimately accomplished.

Introduction

All previous statements concerning the reign or rule of God are now realized. Believers can truly shout:

"Hallelujah! Almighty God, who was and was to come, has taken his great power and *is*."

Remember this is proleptic; it is an announcement of a future event in a vision that John is being shown. We will see shortly that this future event has present significance, not only in John's context but in our own as well.

Text

i) 21:1-4

(1-2) John witnesses all things renewed. The promise of a new heavens and a new earth is a fulfilment of Isaiah 65:17 and 66:22. God's power, love and reality will saturate this world and make it new. Heaven and earth are to be transformed into one, though an everlasting relation and distinction remains in tact through the imagery of bride and bridegroom. In contrast to many Christian notions, where believers are depicted as eternally being with God in heaven, God is going to dwell with his people on earth. He will be in their presence in an utterly new way when renewal finally arrives. This means that our final destiny is to be with God in the new heavens and earth, not to spend forever in the clouds. The statement that there is "no longer any sea" may relate to the ancient idea that the sea was a place of evil. For instance, the beast comes out of the sea (13:1).

As through a telescope we now get a closer view as John sees the Holy City, New Jerusalem, descending from heaven to earth. The city has at least four qualities: it is holy, it is new, it descends out of heaven, and it is from God. These qualities are a radical contrast with what is old in this marvelous, awe-inspiring vision. Beautifully metaphorical, God's city is described as "prepared like a bride dressed for her husband." All these images used are meant to strike us, and to help us take notice of what God is going to do.

(3-4) The proclamation from the throne is that God himself will dwell with his people. This recalls Old Testament imagery when God's temporary dwelling place was the ark and later the temple, but in this context the separation between God and his people was always part of the picture. God draws closer in the New Testament in the person of Christ (Jn. 1:14), and is now present through the Spirit in believers who are called his temple (1 Cor. 6:18-20). God, therefore, does dwell within Christians already through his Spirit to some degree, but the degree of fellowship Christians experience with God will be completely new and wholly transformed. Any distance we experience in reference to fellowship with God will be obliterated. He will wipe away our tears and be forever in our presence. There will be no more death, mourning, crying, or pain. God himself will comfort, heal, and redeem his people. The old order of things has passed away; the new has come and is no longer coming, it is complete.

ii) 21:5-8

(5) No longer does John hear a loud voice speaking from the throne for now it is he who is seated on the throne saying, "I am making everything new." Again there is a present reality of this newness in the life of a Christian. If we are in Christ we are new creations (Jn. 3:4-18; Gal. 6:12-16).

What is evident here, however, is that God's salvific activity includes the political, social, and economic aspects as well as the cosmos itself. John is instructed to write this down for it is trustworthy and true. We can trust God and not lose hope that what he has begun he will surely bring to completion.

(6) God reveals to John, "It is done," or better, "They are done," referring to all the events yet to take place and including the restoration of all things. God is the Alpha and Omega, the beginning and the end. There is no beginning before God and there is no end until he himself brings it about. To those who are thirsty, to those who long for him, to those who recognize their need, he will give drink from the springs of the water of life.

(7) The theme found in this statement is one that has been repeated throughout the Apocalypse, especially in the seven letters (2:1-3:22). Quickly looking at chapters 2:7, 11, 17, 26 and 3:5, 12, 21 shows us the one who overcomes persecution will be rewarded and will inherit the blessings of God and share in his rule. The encouragement to persevere and cling to the victory of Christ is essential to the victory over evil. Those who overcome are promised that God will be their God and that they will be his children, the ultimate sign of adoption and inheritance.

(8) Those who overcome are contrasted with a variety of groups of people who are enemies of God. All these people, for a diversity of reasons, could be considered unbelievers, although they are mentioned here as one group among others. This may lead to the conclusion that cowards and unbelievers, in this context, refers to those who have out rightly renounced their faith in Christ in the midst of persecution, while the others mentioned are pagans or those in churches (2:1-3:22) who join in idolatry and its destruction. In contrast to the inheritance of those who overcome, these will not have a place in the new heavens and earth; their place will be the lake of fire and their inheritance, the second death.

iii) 21:9-21

(9-14) Just as in chapter 17 it was one of the seven angels who showed him the punishment of the great prostitute, it is one of the seven angels who shows John, in the Spirit, the Holy City. Yet again we see a pointed contrast. An idea of what it might be may be found earlier (17:5).

John describes the city as shining with the glory of God, signifying his real presence. In reference to its brilliance, John speaks of it as "like" precious stones. John goes on to describe a great high wall around the city with twelve gates and twelve angels at the gates. The gates have written upon them the names of the twelve tribes of Israel, showing the ongoing significance of the Old Testament people of God and his revelation through them to the nations.

The gates are grouped by three and face in all directions and the twelve foundations of the wall of the city have the names of the twelve apostles. This again affirms the importance of the people through whom God has specifically revealed himself. Note the unity in this: God is King of the world and of Israel in the Old Testament, and his Lamb as the suffering Servant and a messianic ruler is King in the New Testament.

It is important to remember that God reveals himself in *contextual* ways. He is not the static, immutable, impassable God of the Greeks, but the God who chooses to reveal himself in *context*. This means that God is not averse to responding to different situational contexts as they arise. He does so justly, mercifully, in holiness and love *contextually*, although not always or necessarily *simultaneously*. His justice and mercy, as his holiness and love, are not required to be expressed at the same time. God is free to reveal himself in greater or lesser manifestations of his character, without compromising who he is. He can and does choose to be a contextual God, not a static one. Both the Old and New Testaments are important for understanding God's context and both figure into his plan of renewing all things.

(15-21) The new city's measurements are given, emphasizing its perfection and completeness as the dwelling place of God. John continues to describe in further detail, at the very limits of human language, the reality of the Holy City. It is made of pure gold, transparent as glass, with walls of jasper, and visible foundations decorated with a list of precious stones.

The general picture of God's city is one of magnificence, brilliance, purity and the assured rest of completion as all waiting is now translated into the present. In the midst of the great city there will be direct fellowship with God and the Lamb. The 'not yet' will be 'already.' In the literal and figurative sense, blurred vision will be corrected, healed, and brought to perfection. God will dwell with his people, and they with him in everlasting fellowship.

iv) 21:22–27

(22-23) There is no temple in the Holy City because God and the Lamb are its temple. This confirms that direct community with God is available in a deeper, newer, and a more unlimited way, never before experienced by humanity. The city will not need the sun, the temple, or the moon, for God's glory will be its light and the Lamb its lamp. The full presence of God will illumine the world beyond any light which we have known.

(24-27) These verses speak of the universal quality of the knowledge of God. John portrays a picture from the present age into the future, the everlasting. His aim seems to be to point out the comprehensiveness of God's city, where there will be no darkness. John includes the nations in order to depict the greatness of the city and the knowledge of God, to which all nations will bow, as prophesied in the Old Testament (Isa. 52:13-15). The purity of the city is highlighted and those who enter it are they whose names are written in the Lamb's book of life. Access to the city will be denied to all others, demonstrating the city's present character of goodness and everlasting preservation from anything impure.

v) 22:1-5

(1-3) This picture of a river that will nourish the tree of life goes back to the garden in Genesis 2:8-14. The river of the water of life is connected to the giver of life, which originates with God. Life will be sustained and satisfied through the very presence of the Author of life. The tree of life is full of fruit and its leaves are full of healing for the nations. In God's city it will be like living life with no unmet need. Healing will be final in the age to come. Those who have continually struggled, battling a variety of forms of disability and sickness in the present age, will be fully healed. Verse 3 confirms why John continues to contrast the present and future. At this future point there will no longer be any curse. God himself and the Lamb will have their throne in the city, an expression of their rule over the curse, and God's redeemed will have the joy and privilege of serving him. Not only will believers rejoice in being in God's presence, but their service of him, exemplified by completeness, far surpasses any current notions of service.

(4-5) Those who serve God, the redeemed, will see his face. John continues to encourage believers to realize that community with God will be direct, not mediated. This startling new reality is frequently repeated. It is almost as if John cannot believe what he is being shown—the newness is so utterly new. To see God face to face in the Old Testament meant death. Even Moses, in spite of his significant role in salvation history, was not allowed to see God's face. Now those who belong to God, signified here by his name upon their foreheads (14:1), will see him face to face. What a privilege and blessing! John reaffirms that God's presence will be all the light that is necessary; there will be no darkness, and in this light believers will reign forever.

vi) 22:6-11

There is a threefold aim in the following verses, which are frequently referred to as the epilogue. Jesus' words authenticate the prophecy and assert again the certainty of his return, while exhorting and even warning those who read the prophecy to live by it most attentively.

(6) We are reminded a second time that these words are trustworthy and true because they are God's words. This is essential in reference to the origin of what John has written and may be specifically intended to be a powerful reinforcement of this apocalypse in contrast to others of the time.

(7) Also trustworthy is the promise of the risen Lord who announces that he is coming soon. Christians are encouraged to live in this expectancy, even though they do not know the day or the hour. Another beatitude affirms that these words are prophecy and that those who keep them are indeed fortunate. Keeping the words of the prophecy does not mean we are to use them as a complete and detailed guide that explains and articulates the role of particular people or specific events for the future. If the text was intended to be such, it would be hard if not impossible to keep. Rather, I think the point is that the church in every age is called to stand for Christ against Antichrist, to remain steadfast and loyal to him in the midst of pressures and persecution. We may ask ourselves, why? We can answer that question confidently with the truth

that God has faithfully revealed to us the end of history, and the consummation of his rule. His victory is sure, as is ours on the basis of the blood of the Lamb.

(8-9) John again identifies himself and again falls to worship at the feet of an angel as in 19:10. In the face of the constant danger and persistent threat of idolatry, he is strongly warned not to do it. The angel is a fellow servant and not worthy of worship. The exhortation is to worship God and God alone.

(10-11) Verses 10-11 continue to bring us into the present. John must not seal up this prophecy, for the time of its fulfilment is at hand. All must have access to what God has done, is doing, and will do. This admonition is followed by perplexing imperatives for wrong-doers to continue the wrong they are doing and for the righteous to continue to do right.

Do these expressions refer to the fact that the time is near (verse 10) and that Jesus is returning soon (verse 12)? If so, the thought may be that when Jesus arrives there will be some who are persisting in evil and others in holiness. The possibility of changing one's course of action is over; Jesus' return will take place with the speed of the blink of an eye.

Another interpretive option would be to understand the imperatives as a summing up of the attitudes that unbelievers and believers have represented throughout the Apocalypse. There are those who refuse to repent and turn to God, while others bow before him and accept his offer of salvation. Jesus' arrival, not understood by unbelievers, results in arrogant evil acts that continually reject God—so be it—but believers have insight and wisdom concerning Jesus' return, resulting in holy actions continually accepting God—so be it.

vii) 22:12-21

> *"See, I am coming soon! My reward is with me, and I will repay according to everyone's work. I am the Alpha and the Omega, the first and the last, the beginning and the end."*

Jesus' position of divine authority and the abrupt intervention of his coming are underlined. He will draw history to a close at the end of the age, bringing judgement to all and blessing to the righteous. Believers, saved by the blood of Christ, are encouraged to conduct their lives in the light of this salvation and to produce actions in keeping with it, while the stubborn and unrepentant, because of their refusal to accept forgiveness, will reap the consequences of their actions (2:1-3:22).

> *Blessed are those who wash their robes, so that they will have the right to the tree of life and may enter the city by the gates. Outside are the dogs, and sorcerers and fornicators, and murderers, and idolaters, and everyone who loves and practices falsehood.*

These words are both a promise and an exhortation. In spite of adversity, believers are to persevere, as they await Christ's final arrival. They are fortunate as they have blood-washed robes (7:14), which give them rights to the tree of life and entry through the gates into the city. Rich associations of Old Testament imagery from Isaiah 62 and Genesis 3 illumine this passage for the redeemed. Salvation is theirs as they have endured, kept allegiance, and been faithful to the crucified and risen One.

In contrast, there will be those who are excluded. They may claim to have the same vague connection with Christ, but are charlatans and their deceptive actions will betray them. Their ultimate concern is with protecting themselves, not with following the Lamb and all that he stands for.

> *"It is I, Jesus, who sent my angel to you with this testimony for the churches. I am the root and the descendent of David, and the bright morning star."*

> *The Spirit and the bride say, "Come!" And let him who hears say, "Come!" And let everyone who is thirsty, come; let anyone who wishes, take the water of life as a gift.*

The fortitude of Jesus' testimony to those in the churches is unmistakable (1:4, 2:1-3:22). He sends the angel, is the divine light and the fleshly descendent of David (5:5), presenting the composite image of the mighty royal king who will have total and ultimate victory over all his enemies.

As a result of who Jesus is and the testimony he has provided, the Holy Spirit and the corporate true people of God proclaim, "Come" as an invitation to Jesus to bring about the finality of the end.

Next, it is the individuals who hear, which signifies those who believe, to share in the pronouncement and invitation, "Come."

Everyone and anyone who is thirsty are invited to come and partake in the mighty and awesome redemption and salvation that are offered in the present and the end of history.

> *I warn everyone who hears the words of the prophecy of this book: if anyone adds to them, God will add to that person the plagues described in this book; if anyone takes words away from the book of this prophecy, God will take away from that person's share in the tree of life and in the holy city, which are described in this book.*

The highly serious character of John's warning should not be underplayed. In keeping with Old Testament imagery (Deut. 4), to add or take way from these words stresses the danger of making it up as we go along. Inevitably, this results in idolatry, impoverishment, and false teaching. The proliferation of charlatans in our own times highlights the point. False prophets and teachers abound on the landscape of the church, which has often today has lost its way and embraced darkness over light and its own truth versus that which has been revealed.

The one who testifies to these things says, "Surely I am coming soon." Amen. Come, Lord Jesus.

The sober warning of the previous verses is rooted in Jesus—the one who testifies to these things. All of what has been testified to in the Apocalypse is valued and sure testimony that what has been revealed is coming to pass. John, who has seen and written, and those who hear and read can only respond, "Amen. Come, Lord Jesus."

The grace of the Lord Jesus be with all the saints. Amen.

SELECT BIBLIOGRAPHY

Allo, E. B. *L'Apocalypse* (Paris: Gabalda, 3e ed. 1933).

Aune, D. E. *The New Testament in Its Literary Environment* (Philadelphia: Westminster, 1987).

Aune, D. E. *Revelation* (Dallas, Nashville: Word/Nelson, 1997-1998).

Bauckham, R. *The Climax of Prophecy* (Edinburgh: T & T Clark, 1993).

Beale, G. K. *The Book of Revelation* (Grand Rapids, Carlisle: Eerdmans/Paternoster, 1999).

Beasley-Murray, G. R. *The Book of Revelation* (London: Marshall, Morgan, Scott, 1974).

Beckwith, I. T. *The Apocalypse of John* (Grand Rapids: Baker, 2nd print. 1967).

Caird, G. B. *The Revelation of St John the Divine* (Peabody: Hendrickson, 1987).

Charles, R. H. *A Critical and Exegetical Commentary on the Revelation of St John* (Edinburgh: T & T Clark, 1920).

Ford, J. M. *Revelation* (New York: Doubleday, 1975).

Hemer, C. J. *The Letters to the Seven Churches in Asia* (Sheffield: Sheffield Academic Press, 1986).

Ladd, G. E. *A Commentary on the Revelation of John* (Grand Rapids: Eerdmans, 1972).

Metzger, B. M. *Breaking the Code: Understanding the Book of Revelation* (Nashville: Abingdon, 1993).

Morris, L. *The Book of Revelation* (Leicester: Intervarsity Press, 1969).

Mounce, R. H. *The Book of Revelation* (Grand Rapids: Eerdmans, 1977).

Mulholland, M. R. *Revelation* (Grand Rapids: Zondervan, 1990).

Peterson, E. H. *Reversed Thunder* (San Francisco: HaperCollins, 1988).

Prigent, P. *Apocalypse et liturgie* (Neuchâtel : Delachaux et Niestle, 1964).

Prigent, P. *L'Apocalypse de Saint Jean* (Genève : Labor et Fides, 1988).

Rowland, C. *The Open Heaven* (London: SPCK, 1985).

Schaeffer, F.A. *Revelation* (Huémoz, tapes, 1970).

www.ingramcontent.com/pod-product-compliance
Lightning Source LLC
Chambersburg PA
CBHW022012290426
44109CB00015B/1151